Self-Publishing

Self-Publishing

A guide to publishing your own book
from first draft to release day

Emma Rosen

Sartain
Publishing

Published by Sartain Publishing Ltd, Canterbury
www.sartainpublishing.co.uk

Edited by Kim Kimber
www.kimkimber.co.uk

Cover illustrations by Steve 'Squidoodle' Turner
www.squidoodleshop.com

978-1-915289-00-1

For Stuart.
I simply couldn't do this without you.

About the Author

Emma Rosen and her husband live in Kent and have three adorable children and a silly dog.

After ten years as a biology teacher, Emma now focuses entirely on writing, with particular interests in marine ecology, early parenting and independent publishing. She has degrees in marine biology and in education.

Emma is passionate about breastfeeding and volunteers as a peer supporter at a local group. When she's not writing or having fun with her family, Emma makes YouTube videos, spends time by the sea and sings in a band.

www.emmarosenbooks.co.uk

Contents

Introduction

If you're reading this, it means you have either written a book or you are deep into the process. This is an enormous accomplishment, and you should give yourself a huge pat on the back before we even start. However, in many ways, the journey has only just begun. Now it's time to turn your writing into a tangible product.

I have written this book to share my knowledge from self-publishing my own books. I've shared my experience of publishing on my YouTube channel (as well as my love of books) and have now amassed over a hundred videos. Every day I receive messages asking me questions about the process and I regularly share tips and signpost information. I'm passionate about supporting other writers going through this process and you'll find a lot of useful information here – I know I would have found it helpful when I started.

When I wrote my first book, I hadn't planned a publishing process – I was just astonished to have finished writing! I did pursue traditional publishing, for a time, with no luck and I found it a demoralising experience. Once I turned my attention to self-publishing, all the excitement about my project came rushing back. I decided to forget about the traditional route entirely. Self-publishing gave me creative control; I had complete ownership of every aspect of my 'book baby' and I loved it.

Of course, it's not that simple – I knew it would undoubtedly involve a lot of hard work and stress. But, looking back, it's been completely worth it. So worth it, in fact, that I've continued my career as an independent author.

So, that's how this book originated. These pages contain everything I've learned (together with a few new things I've researched to make sure this book really does have *everything* in it!). Over the following pages I will be covering the stages you'll go through to get your book out into the world. Whether you read this book from cover to cover in one go, or each section as you need it, you'll find a lot of information to help you publish your own book. So, let's dive in!

Author's note

All the information in this book is up-to-date at the time of publication but be sure to check specific details when you're making decisions. As a British writer, I will occasionally focus more on options or resources within the UK, but there are generally similar alternatives in other territories.

Why Self-Publish?

At one time, my fantasy of 'becoming' a writer was signing a book deal in the swanky London office of a prestigious publisher. I would be consulted about the important decisions (perhaps insisting dramatically on my own creative ideas) but, mostly, I would just sit back while someone else did the work and wait for the money to roll in. I am aware this is not how traditional publishing really looks – but a girl can dream...

When it comes to it, your romanticised version of book publishing may not be the actual road you choose to go down (and, like mine, it may not really exist). So, it's important to explore your options in order to make the right choices for you and your book.

Securing a book deal is *hard*. In order to be traditionally published you have to be fortunate enough to find a publisher that wants to invest in your book. In the current climate, many people who obtain publishing deals already have a following; perhaps they're an expert in their field or they have a large social media audience. This doesn't mean your creative work shouldn't be published; it means that a company may not be willing to invest in it as they are less likely to make a profit than with an established personality. It may be that you're coming to self-publishing after being turned down – and that's OK!

Self-publishing is not what it was. There used to be a degree of stigma attached to it. However, with the advent of ebooks and easy internet access there's been a flood of self-published work. Of course, the quality is variable, and I think that's where the negativity came from. Anyone can put content out but not all of it is good. Nonetheless, self-publishing is a viable and professional route to follow. It's an option that many people choose as a preference – not because they didn't get a book deal, not because they're just 'putting their book on the internet', but because they *want* to publish that way. Now there's even more potential as print publishing has become easier. With the advent of print on demand (POD) services there's no need for storage space and you don't have to guess how many books you will sell, perhaps only to end up hauling them to the tip in a few years' time if you grossly miscalculated.

Some writers prefer to traditionally publish, others to self-publish and some do a bit of both. Some try one and then move to the other. It really depends on you, your book and your preferences. In this chapter I'm going to run through the main pros and cons of each. If you're still making a decision, this may help you to choose the best option for you.

Choosing to publish

Self-publishing makes the decision to publish your manuscript *yours*. If you think your book deserves to be read, publish it. You don't need the endorsement of someone else; it's completely your decision.

Control

In my opinion, the biggest advantage of self-publishing is control. Even if you work with other professionals during this process, ultimately every decision comes back to you. You decide if you want to include a certain passage in your book, what the cover will look like, what formats the book will be available in, when it will be released, pricing, marketing strategy...everything. It's all you.

In traditional publishing many of those decisions will occur entirely without your input, although, if you're lucky, you might get a say. On the other hand, that means the workload is taken from your shoulders and you also benefit from the knowledge of people with industry experience. That might appeal to you. But if you prefer to see your own vision through to the end, then self-publishing may be a better option.

Time frame

Traditional publishing takes a long time. To begin with, it's a long process to find an agent (if you choose to work with one; you don't have to but many publishers will only deal with agents). Then, it can take months to place your book with a publisher. Many prefer you not to submit your manuscript to multiple companies, so you're forced to wait while each slowly considers your fate. Publishers are notoriously swamped with submissions. Ultimately, at the end of that lengthy process, it might still be a 'no'.

Self-publishing is considerably quicker. You could be holding your book in your hands in a matter of weeks. For some writers this allows their book to stay current, rather than being out-of-date before it's even released. For others it saves a lot of frustration waiting for someone to take a chance on you. It's undeniable that this is a big advantage in self-publishing.

Expense

If you pursue the traditional route, the publisher will foot the bill for the costs associated with the book. Sometimes, you receive an advance. If your book earns back that money, you begin to receive royalties. If your book isn't profitable enough, you may find future book deals are more lean. Still, the money should be coming in rather than out. In self-publishing, on the other hand, *you* have to invest. If it all goes wrong, it will be you that's out of pocket.

Another way to view it is that you're able to decide how much money to invest in the book and, therefore, at which point the book begins to be profitable. This gives you greater financial control over the return on investment and the focus of spending.

Be suspicious of any publisher that expects you to invest your own money. Be sure that they will make a professional job of your book and market it; many hybrid and vanity publishers (as these are known) are more interested in making money than publishing.

Royalties

As a self-published author you should be getting a higher royalty rate on your books. After all, the royalties are all yours! Traditionally published authors have to split their royalties with their publisher and agent. You also get paid more regularly than a traditionally published author; they may only be paid biannually whereas print on demand services typically pay out monthly (although there is a time-lag of up to 90 days after sales).

Workload

It's true that traditional publishing is less work for the author. The publishing house will handle the bulk of the production and marketing. Of course, you need to factor in the time spent querying agents and/or publishers, but still, you are going to have to commit a lot of time and effort to the publishing process if you want to self-publish professionally. If time is an issue, consider using a 'self-publishing service' to handle a proportion of the work.

Marketing

As above, a traditional publishing house will market your book – probably. Often they invest more in 'big' titles (those that guarantee greater revenue) while other books receive a lot less of the marketing budget. However, they have a recognised brand and a reach that's extremely hard to achieve as a self-published author. If you self-publish, you will have to handle your own marketing (I discuss ideas later in this book).

Again, this is perhaps dependent on how you frame it. I enjoy digital marketing and I've had fun learning this side of the publishing business (and there's a lot to it!). But more to the point, I've also been able to choose how to advertise. It's entirely possible to be traditionally published and feel unhappy with how your book has been promoted or find it hasn't really been marketed at all (something to look out for if you are choosing a traditional publisher).

Changes

Self-publishing authors typically use POD services. Although they may hold a small amount of stock to sell from home, they're often not printing runs of thousands of copies. Therefore, if you notice a typo down the line, you can change it, practically immediately! In traditional publishing this is extremely hard to do. They would still need to sell the old stock even if there's an error.

For this reason, self-publishing is particularly well-suited to a changing field. If you're writing about a subject where information tends to change, it's quick and easy to make alterations and ensure your book is up-to-date.

Sales

If you self-publish, unfortunately, you're likely to have much lower sales. You probably don't have access to as large an audience as a publishing house. You don't have the same branding and reach as someone established in the industry. This is definitely an important point to consider. You might make more money per book, but you will probably sell fewer copies. It would be remiss of me not to highlight this point – it's entirely possible to not sell enough copies to pay off your investment, especially if you're just starting out. It's a definite downside and one that requires careful consideration.

Quality

Throughout this book we will discuss ways to ensure your book is of a professional standard. However, one of the downsides to self-publishing is the potential to produce an amateur book. Perhaps it's not as well-written as the industry expects or maybe it's poorly edited. It could be that there are problems with the layout or the cover is basic. You don't have the same experience or expertise as the industry experts and, if you're not careful, it will show. This is important in all your decision-making – make sure your book is as professional as possible. Working with freelance professionals can really help in this respect.

One thing to note is that reviews are your friend. They are your quality assurance as a self-published author. Good reviews help reassure a potential readership who might be unsure about a self-published author (although, if you've done your job well, they might not even know).

I call myself an independent or 'indie' author, as do many self-published authors. What's the difference? Well, it is a little grey, but I see it as a mindset shift, and it's all about professionalism. For an indie, writing is a business. Their books are professional products. Whether it's a side-hustle or a career, independent authors take things seriously. For this reason, indie authors typically employ freelancers (again, more on this later) to add their expertise to the project. Indies generally emulate the standards set by traditional publishers. Some self-published authors may not view their project in quite the same way but many do. As I say, the definition is muddy: some indies don't use freelancers all the time; some self-published authors produce higher-quality books than indies. Whatever you call it, I think it's useful to view yourself as I do – someone who is looking to publish as professional a product as they can with the budget they have available.

* * *

I hope you've read all that and feel self-publishing is for you (after all, you've picked up this book). It's exciting to be the person in charge and you can have a great deal of fun learning about the publishing process and making creative decisions. You get to bring your book baby into the world yourself!

Of course, you may decide you don't want to self-publish – and that's fine. However, if you feel that way, please don't put this book down without reading to the end; you may feel differently once you see what's involved. If you decide to go the traditional route after all, I suggest you take a look at *The Writers' and Artists' Yearbook* (or similar publications outside of the UK) to find a list of agents and publishers, along with great tips on the whole process.

Over the coming pages I will guide you through the various stages of publishing your own book. You've got a lot of decisions to make and new skills to learn. After all, you're now the managing director of your new publishing empire.

Resources

The Writers' and Artists' Yearbook: www.writersandartists. co.uk

Planning

Take a moment to plan out the production of your book; you will be more organised and it will make your decision-making easier. It's a good idea to research your options and make decisions about the route you plan to take rather than approaching the process haphazardly. Things may change along the way, but you will be more prepared to handle any challenges you meet.

I recently found the notebook where I'd scribbled my thoughts and research when I published my first book. It was an odd little window into the start of the process for me. Admittedly, I'm a list maker and I love a fancy notebook, but I recommend you write down your plans in a format that suits you so you can refer back to it as you go.

So, read through this book and access online resources to help you expand your knowledge. Then start to formulate a publishing plan for the coming months.

Set a goal

It's important to establish what your goal is. It may seem obvious – you want to publish a book – but everybody has a different motivation and that may affect how you approach the project.

Perhaps you simply want your book in print. You need to see the words in black and white and feel the weight of the paper in your hands. It's less important how many copies you sell and how much profit you make; rather, you simply want this book out in the world. If you feel this way, you may be more likely to spend a larger sum of money on bringing your creative vision to reality and it's important to remember to balance that with the potential return on investment.

Maybe you're looking to launch yourself into writing as a career, so that it becomes your main source of income. For you, the focus will be profit. The book is a product that forms a part of the business you're building. Your focus is more likely to be on minimising costs and maximising sales, as well as building a future audience for more books or other aspects of your business.

You might be more interested in accolades. Perhaps it's vital for you to hit the Amazon bestseller lists. If this is you, then your focus is going to be on selling as many copies as possible, and selling them through the right outlets. Maybe you dream of your book winning 'Self-Published Book of the Year' (that award doesn't exist – but maybe it should!).

You will more likely to focus on the artistic value of your writing. If you're interested in winning awards, you should research those that fit your book genre and start applying. Do remember that self-published authors aren't eligible for certain awards, unfortunately.

For many of us, it will be a mixture, and something that evolves. The important thing, however, is to know what your main priorities are. This helps you to decide where to invest your time and money and where you may be willing to take workarounds. Decide what your vision is for the future and what you want to achieve. It can change, of course, as you learn more about the process, but it gives you a great starting point when you're planning.

Budget

As I said in the last chapter, being self-published means you have to invest your own money, and this brings a whole new angle to the project. It's really important to decide on your budget so that you use your money wisely.

Realistically, self-publishing can be expensive. You can spend anything between a few hundred pounds to a few thousand, depending on the decisions you make. As you do your research you will need to consider the cost implications (often there are multiple options with different associated costs). Knowing your budget and then allocating that to stages of the publishing process (keeping your goals in mind) will help you to plan your route.

Firstly, what can you afford? My personal opinion is to think about this investment as money you will not see back again. It's a risk you've taken and whether it returns or not is unknown at present. That may seem defeatist, but if you ultimately struggle to sell books – can you afford to lose this money? The last thing you want is to risk the finances necessary to run your personal life because you invested in a project that didn't work out. So, while we naturally remain optimistic that you will make sales – how much money can you afford to lose if the worst happens?

Of course, you have to speculate to accumulate. You *will* have to invest, and doing this wisely will make your book more successful. So, be prepared to spend on the important aspects of publishing in order to create a professional and competitive product.

If you want to minimise the personal financial risk, or if money is tight, you could fund the book through crowdfunding. A commonly used option is Kickstarter. If you're unfamiliar with this crowdfunding platform, it's certainly worth taking a look. You set a monetary target and offer rewards for people who invest – usually copies of the book and associated merchandise. Set a realistic target for your audience size so that the funds will be released to you (if you don't reach your target, you don't get the money). Add some brilliant bonuses to incentivise investment and then advertise your Kickstarter hard. This also helps to advertise your book while you're still creating it. Once you have the money, use it wisely and make sure you deliver on those rewards!

Once you've established how much you have to spend (including any crowdfunding campaigns you plan to run), think about how to use your budget in the best way to achieve your goals. As you read through this book you might have to adjust the figure you were prepared to spend as you realise the costs associated with self-publishing to a professional standard.

Set a timeline

Every project will look different, and it's a good idea to know what work needs to be completed and when. As you read through the following chapters, think about how you're going to go about each aspect and how long it will take. Factor in your other commitments – how much time can you realistically give to the project around your everyday life? If it takes you longer, but fits in comfortably to your life, that's quite alright! For my first book I gave myself approximately six months to publish (you can set longer timescales if it suits you). For my second I ended up doing much of the production work in a month – I know which was preferable!

Use this book as a guide to the steps you need to schedule. You won't necessarily follow the stages in this book in the same order, but it gives you an idea of how to work through the process logically. You will probably find certain elements overlap. You're likely to be working on something while a freelancer works on another aspect, and we all multitask to an extent. Take this into account; decide how you want to progress, and set out your deadlines accordingly. If you're not sure how long each task will take, ask other writers and freelancers. You can get estimates of timescale as well as availability which will help to build your plan.

Once you have an idea of the timescales, schedule in deadlines for each aspect of the publishing process. You should end up with everything completed at least six to eight weeks before the release date to allow plenty of time to market the book. When you set your release date, perhaps look at the calendar for any significant dates; it can be fun to tie in your book launch with a national celebration day or a local event. Or, maybe you have a big selling opportunity and you want to ensure your book is released in time.

One of the beauties of self-publishing is that you have the flexibility to change the publication date if things aren't going to schedule, although once you've publicised it, changes become difficult for your customer base. However, in the early stages, you can be more flexible as you learn what is involved.

My biggest tip is to allow wiggle room! Add in time buffers wherever possible, especially the first time around. You're learning a new process, there are bound to be setbacks. You might not like the designs your cover designer comes up with or your editor might find more errors than you realised. Then there's always the risk that something unforeseen happens in your personal life that requires your attention. It's always better to enjoy the publishing process than for it to be a strain. Don't work to extremely tight deadlines, add in spare weeks along the way and allow a big chunk of marketing time. You don't want to have to rush any part; be realistic and kind to yourself.

There are lots of different ways to visualise this plan. Maybe you simply write the dates on your calendar or you might create a full-on Gantt chart; but find a way of representing what you need to do that works. Personally, I'm a list maker. I write out what requires doing, with dates next to it and tick it off. It's that simple!

Resources

Kickstarter: www.kickstarter.com

Business

Before we get into the technical aspects of creating your book, you should consider the business side of things. In creating a product and selling it you are, inevitably, creating a business.

Now, this company can be as big or small as you like. It can also have any structure you want. It largely depends on how you see the publishing of your book and your future within the industry. If you're publishing one book, keep it simple. If this is your new career, you may like to think about something more substantial. You can, of course, change as you grow. Over the next pages I will go through a few of your options and the points you need to consider.

Branding

As a self-published author, you will also essentially be a publisher. It can help to make things look professional if you have a publishing company name and logo on your book. It also means that when you list your book for sale it doesn't say 'independently published' under the publisher name, but rather whatever company name you've come up with (provided you have your own ISBNs). My company is called Sartain Publishing Ltd, which simply uses my maiden name. I thought it was a good way to have the name I grew up with incorporated into my creative life.

If you wish, have fun coming up with a name and logo. You can even design your own (I got a friend to do it) or pay a designer, but keep it simple as it will be very small on your book.

Setting up a company

Sole trader/sole proprietorship

It will probably suit most people to function as a sole trader. This type of company does not require registration. You will, however, need to register for self-assessment and file a tax return every year as well as keeping records of your income and expenditure. In general, this is a simple type of company to run. You keep any profits, and losses can be carried over. However, the name of your company is not protected in the same way, so if you have branding associated to this, you may wish to investigate registering for copyright.

If you're setting up your business as a partnership it follows similar rules (dependent on territory). You will have to register as a partnership with one of you being the nominated partner that deals with the tax return and other paperwork.

Limited company/corporation

You may prefer to set up a more formal company. A limited company is likely to be most suitable, where you (and anyone else you wish) are a director and shareholder. This keeps the company legally separate from your own finances, which offers you some protection. You're paid through dividends, which generally attract a lower tax rate. You might also wish to pay yourself a salary on top of this if your profits are sufficient.

In the UK, if you form a limited company, you will need to choose a name that has not already been used by another company and, once you're registered, that name is protected. You will have to register with Companies House and your name and address is listed on their website. For that reason, you might prefer to pay for a 'brass plate' company and use their address in order to protect your own (in other countries you may be able to use a PO Box, check local rules).

As the managing director of a limited company you will not only have to complete a tax return for your own income, but also a company return as well as filing company accounts (this information is viewable on the internet). There is also a yearly fee to remain registered.

Forming a limited company requires a lot more paperwork, but protects your company name. It will also be advantageous tax-wise if you reach a certain level of profit due to the reduced tax rates for dividend payouts. If you can handle the paperwork (or afford to pay an accountant to help you), this may be a route to consider.

Again, all this will depend on the vision you have for your business. If you are releasing one book and expecting a low income, a sole trader company will be just fine. However, if you have a longer-term plan, or if your company has started to earn more money, a limited company may suit you better.

Bank account

When you sell your books, any income you make should be declared for tax reasons. It's advisable to separate your money for your books from your personal finances. If you're keeping things small, you could use a separate personal account that has no other transactions.

At some point, you may want to consider a business account (I have found a few companies I've dealt with require one, although most don't). Most business accounts incur monthly fees and many also charge for transactions. Free periods of banking are often available for startups and sometimes if you switch accounts. Some banks also don't charge if you have a certain amount of money in the account. Shop around and find something that meets your requirements.

All this needs to be considered in terms of legality, what income you're expecting and your banking requirements. However, the most important thing is keeping the money from your business separate and keeping records.

Resources

These are UK specific; other territories will have similar information and resources, usually accessible from your government website.

The UK Copyright Service: copyrightservice.co.uk
Companies House: www.gov.uk/government/
  organisations/companies-house
HMRC: www.gov.uk/government/organisations/hm-
  revenue-customs

ISBNs

A lot of people seem to get confused about ISBNs – it's one of the things I receive the most questions about. Therefore, I'm going to explain your options before moving on.

ISBN stands for International Standard Book Number. It consists of a unique 13 digit code that identifies your book. ISBNs are used by publishers, booksellers and libraries to order, catalogue and sell books. If you publish without an ISBN (for example if you're just ordering a few copies of a book to give to friends), you seriously limit the options for your book.

Each format requires a separate ISBN, so paperback, hardback and large print will each require a different number. Audiobooks and ebooks are a little more complex. If you publish directly through a platform, you will probably find they allocate their own identification code, unique to their system. Therefore, if you only publish through them, you won't require an ISBN. Their code does not need to appear anywhere in your book, it will simply be on their website. If you use aggregators (who distribute your book to multiple sites), they will need an ISBN as this unifies the records from all the different services.

Have a look at the requirements of the platforms you want to use and that will inform you on how many ISBNs you will need. To clarify, you do not require different ISBNs for each platform you use, only for each format. So for example, if you use two platforms for your paperback, you give them both the same number.

There are a few options on how to obtain ISBNs, which I will outline below.

Obtain them for free

Several self-publishing platforms offer free ISBNs if your book is exclusive to them – and some of these are wide distributors (meaning your book will be available through multiple outlets). The big advantage to this is financial; it's one less cost to worry about and one less step you have to do yourself. However, it limits your options if you wish to move your book to a different platform at a later date. It also means your book will not carry your publishing name on its listings (it will probably say 'independently published' or similar). Be aware that using free ISBNs provided by self-publishing platforms will prevent some shops stocking your books. Check with shops you hope to work with if this may influence your decision.

Buy your own

If you would prefer to own your ISBNs, you will need to buy them. In some countries ISBNs are free but, in general, you should purchase them through the national provider in your territory; for example, Nielsen in the UK and Bowker in the USA. You can find your agency through ISBN International if you're not sure. ISBNs are typically available singly or in bundles of 10, 100 or 1000, so you need to buy the quantity that suits your requirements. There is a price benefit in buying more, so if you know you will use more in the future it's worth buying a larger amount. Interestingly, the numerical identifiers in the ISBN show how many you bought (if you know what to look for) and so some people can guess whether you're self-published or traditionally-published by looking at your ISBN.

If you have decided to create a publishing company, you should buy your ISBNs using that company name. They will then be linked to your company and that will show in the metadata. Once you've purchased your ISBNs you should receive a list of them in an email. If you've bought more than one, keep a record of which ones you use and for what title and format.

As you publish books and/or make changes you need to notify your agency (Nielsen Title Editor in the UK, Books in Print in the US) and make amendments online. You may also have to fill in information that hasn't been automatically updated when your book was published. For me, my name hadn't been listed in the record for one ISBN, making it difficult for booksellers to find my books. It's important to ensure all the metadata is correct and that it matches the information on your publishing platform. Discrepancies can cause issues with orders and searchability so always check your records and ensure everything is correct and update it if you make changes.

Barcodes

Some companies offer packages of barcodes for your print editions. Generally, these are not necessary. Some platforms, such as Kindle Direct Publishing (KDP), can add their own barcode and you simply leave a space in the area they specify when you're designing the cover. Others require you to include a barcode, but you can either crop them out of the cover templates (this is what I do for Ingram Spark) or use online barcode generators.

Resources

ISBN International: www.isbn-international.org
Bowker: www.bowker.com
Nielsen: www.nielsenisbnstore.com
Nielsen Title Editor: www.nielsentitleeditor.com
Books in Print: www.booksinprint.com

Editing

This book isn't a guide to writing (look for craft books for help with that), so I'm going to jump in at the editing phase. Firstly, I have to make it clear that *you must edit your book*! I cannot emphasise this enough. Too many self-published books go out without sufficient editing and it's the number one thing that will make your book amateurish in my opinion.

Editing isn't the most exciting process in the world, but it's completely necessary. It is something that you get better at, and I personally get quite absorbed in it these days (with a bit of background music for a creative atmosphere). You'll find your own way to tackle all the facets of perfecting your manuscript.

A whole book could be dedicated to editing. In fact, a whole book could be given to a lot of the sections in this book. But, in this chapter, I am going to explain the different options for editing, from self-editing to working with professionals. This can be an extremely costly part of the process but that doesn't mean you should skip it. Your book may require significant money spent on it and that's something you will need to assess and accept.

Self-editing

This first stage is so important. Your book needs to be the best you can make it before you progress any further. The more editing you do yourself, the more money you will save on professional editing (as they will have less to do).

It's helpful to completely finish your draft before starting to edit so you aren't sidetracked. You can end up in a seemingly endless circle of writing and editing the same sections. Get the words on the page and start editing afterwards.

You might find the following techniques and tips useful during the self-editing phase.

Read it...and then read it again

Start by repeatedly reading through the text. You can break it down into sections to make it easier, but you're probably going to read your entire book enough times to be able to recite it by heart, or at least it feels that way. You may even start to hate your own writing, but it's all just part of the process. Go over and over your work until it's as near perfect as possible, no matter how much it starts to annoy you.

Print it out

A pen-and-paper edit is an excellent method to use. You also get to see the manuscript as a physical thing (for the first time, for most of us).

Much of my editing is done on my laptop. However, at a certain stage I feel I need a colourful pen and a manuscript in a folder. 'Marking' my book has a different feel for me than editing on-screen. Perhaps it's because of my past life as a teacher, but I pick up different issues and I find myself writing notes that I otherwise might not follow up. For me, it also means I can edit in different places than I would if working on my laptop; for example, I used to take my editing to my children's swimming lessons.

At intervals, go back to your working document and type up your changes. Don't leave this too long or you might find your notes have become cryptic.

Read it backwards

This might sound a little crazy, but reading your text from right to left, or bottom to top, helps you to spot typos and repeated words because you're no longer paying attention to content.

Read it aloud

I find reading aloud one of the best self-editing tools. When you read the book out loud, you suddenly spot all the words that don't fit (for example, those that repeat or sound out-of-place). It becomes clear which sentences don't flow. You also find sections that don't make sense or lack clarity. You will automatically stumble over the parts that don't work.

You could also read the book aloud to someone trusted – and perhaps get their input. It depends how you feel about seeing their reactions. Personally, I prefer to read it alone. If you feel self-conscious talking to yourself, you could read your book to your pets. Do whatever works for you – but reading out loud is a great way to edit.

If you're thinking of recording an audiobook (which I'm not covering this time), this is a good opportunity to discover the parts that seem fine on the page but don't work so well when read aloud.

Listen to your book

If you have a willing friend, ask them to read your book to you. Hearing someone else read your story helps you to see where they stumble over sections that seemed fine to you. You will also receive the story differently from when you read it yourself, and it may highlight issues you didn't spot before. In the fairly-likely scenario that other people are too busy or unwilling, consider using software to read your book to you. Both Mac and Windows have narration tools that you could use.

What to look for

Getting your book written down is only half the battle. Polishing it up is a whole different situation. Now you're looking at it more critically than creatively.

While you are editing there are several important things you should be looking for. Some writers prefer to address each aspect in separate edits, others go more haphazardly, but the important thing is to ensure you have checked the whole document for each element. You will probably discover you have particular issues. For example, I use the word 'that' far too much.

Tips to consider as you run through your story:

- *Spelling:* Look out for typos and misuse of words (there/their/they're or advice/advise, for example).

- *Grammar:* Are your sentences correctly structured?

- *Punctuation:* Look for consistent use of punctuation. Ensure you've used commas and colons correctly. If you're not sure, you may have to research certain points; punctuation can be complicated! Grammarly can be a helpful tool.

- *Word use:* Could you have used a better word? Look out for boring words or ones that just don't flow. Use a thesaurus and have a play. Don't go overboard though; sometimes keeping it simple is best.

- *Repeated words:* Do you have a favourite word? Don't keep using it! Also, do a search through your document for use of 'that'. If you can remove it from the sentence and it still makes sense, then do so. Repeat the process for 'very': 'very big' is huge, 'very beautiful' is stunning, 'very upset' is devastated...you get the idea.

- *Show, don't tell:* This is a big one for fiction and narrative non-fiction writers. If you find you're telling the reader everything rather than showing them, your story will be boring. For example, 'She felt upset' vs 'a tear rolled silently down her face'.

- *Info-dumping:* If you've written a whole paragraph of description, probably don't. Try to world-build gradually. It is possible to describe a character without saying what each person is wearing as they're introduced. Try to be subtle.

- *Story:* Does your story make sense? Have you accidentally mentioned something before introducing it?

- *Timeline:* Make sure your timeline works. Nobody should be travelling 200 miles by horse in an hour. Are your characters suddenly in a place they couldn't possibly be? Was it night a minute ago and now it's day?

- *Fact check:* If you wrote something in your draft and you weren't sure it was right, check it. Depending on what you're writing, you may have to reference it. I find the Chicago style of referencing works well in books.

- *Dialogue tags:* More often than not, just use 'said'. Too much exalting, hissing, stating and pronouncing gets annoying. Enough said (pun intended).

- *Passive voice:* Try to edit out passive voice – the subject should be central to the sentence. For example, 'the letter was delivered by my uncle yesterday' is better written as 'my uncle delivered the letter yesterday'.

- *Phrases:* Popular or vernacular phrases should be avoided in books. For instance, phrases like 'don't cry over spilled milk' or 'saved my bacon' may not be used in all lexicons.

* * *

Once you're happy with your manuscript it's time to get fresh eyes on it. Other people may view it differently and experts will spot things you've never dreamed of.

Critique partners

You might choose to work with a partner during writing and/or editing. A critique partner is someone you share your work with for feedback and they do the same with you. You learn from each other and help one another through the process. They can be critical about your writing and can be someone to bounce ideas off. A critique partner can cheer you on through the process. You support one another as writers. This is a good option if you find you feel insular, and you prefer to work with colleagues. This will look different for all critique partners, but if you have a writer friend who is always willing to look over a chapter or have a chat with you about your work – you have a critique partner.

Beta readers

Beta readers are a bit like beta testers – they're trying your book out. You can recruit beta readers via social media, or you could use people you know (although they may be less honest). Look for beta readers that are a good fit for your project: people who read the genre you are writing or people with relevant expertise (for instance, a breastfeeding counsellor read *Milk*, my breastfeeding book). Look for readers who fit your audience: a children's book needs to be tested by kids. Women's literature should be read by women. Although you may wish a range of people to read your book, ensure you have covered your core demographic.

You should also consider using sensitivity readers. Diversity in books is important, but inaccuracies and stereotypes are unhelpful. A sensitivity reader can look over any representation within your book including race, class, sexuality and disability. For example, if you've written an LGBTQ+ character and you're not part of that community, ask an LGBTQ+ person to read it and provide feedback.

To maximise feedback from beta readers, think about giving them specific questions about each section or big picture ones about the whole book. Ensure they know they can be honest; it's better to have their negative opinions now than bad reviews in the future. It's important to listen to your beta readers and take their comments on board, otherwise there is little point in using them. Evaluate their comments and use the ones that help your manuscript to be better.

Beta readers usually do not get paid, but a thank you in the acknowledgements and a free book goes a long way.

Professional editors

Professional editing is expensive (although the fee varies depending on the length of your book and your time frame). This does not mean you shouldn't have your manuscript professionally edited. There are several different types of editor and it's for you to decide the kind of editing your book requires and tie that in with what you can afford. If, for financial reasons, you choose not to hire a professional editor then you must ensure you have edited your work to the highest standard possible and that you have had other eyes on your work. Remember to thank the owners of those eyes for helping you to edit for free. However, I *highly* recommend you work with a professional.

Rates for editing will vary, but make sure you know what is typically charged. The Chartered Institute of Editors and Proofreaders (CIEP) currently set minimum hourly rates at £34.40 for developmental or substantive editing, £29.90 for copy-editing and £25.70 for proofreading. However, you might not necessarily need all of these forms of editing; you should decide which of them would benefit your book. There is some overlap between the types of editing, and you will find that a line editor will flag up typos and a copy-editor will point out parts of your story that don't make sense. However, it's about focus and specialism: where do you require help the most? (And everybody needs some help!) Ensure you have carefully researched the editor you are using so you get the most out of your money.

Editors are likely to edit the manuscript on a word processor using track changes and add comments where necessary. You can then run through their edits and either accept or reject them. It's a simple system that's easy to use.

Developmental editing

Everybody has to start somewhere, and you might find that you're struggling to get your story out. Even experienced writers may want help tightening a plot. Whether you're having difficulty making the plot work, your story isn't exciting enough or your characters are two dimensional, a developmental editor can help with all of that.

Developmental editors specialise in story-telling, so if you feel your story is flat, you should consider hiring one to suggest ways to improve your early drafts. Not all books require a developmental editor, but if you're finding it hard, hiring a professional might help you to move forward and you will learn a lot from them.

Substantive editing

Similarly, substantive editing focusses on the bigger picture. A substantive editor looks at how your book is laid out and organised. They will also address things like pacing and clarity and examine overall language use and tone. Ultimately, they hone your book to achieve its goals and best suit its readers.

Line editing

A line editor looks at language and style at a paragraph level. They assess whether the words you have used work well creatively and stylistically. They will also look at the clarity of your work and whether your writing is conveying what you want to say.

Copy-editing

Copy-editors will point out spelling, grammar, punctuation and syntax issues according to suitable guides. They are specialists in the mechanics of language.

Proofreading

Proofreading is the final stage of editing. A proofreader will check for any remaining mistakes in spelling and grammar. Ideally, proofreading should take place after your book has been designed so the proofreader can also look out for things like widow or orphan lines (where the start or end of a paragraph hangs awkwardly over into the next page), page numbering errors or design mistakes such as repeated pages or sections.

Securing an editor

You may find many of the descriptions from previous pages used interchangeably. Some editors separate copy and line editing, others don't. Sometimes developmental and substantive work is grouped together. For this reason, make sure you're clear exactly what you want an editor to do with your book and communicate that.

When choosing freelancers, you need to ensure they are going to do a good, professional job. You don't want to be disappointed in the quality or amount of work your editor does, or to discover your money is gone and little or no editing has been done. You should aim to work with somebody you 'vibe' with, as you don't want to hire an editor who annoys you or makes you feel criticised. The best author-editor relationship is one where you learn from working with them while making your book the best it can be.

Of course, you can browse the internet to find an editor, but a good place to start is with a registered professional body. In the UK, I would recommend the CIEP. They have a keyword search option to help you find editors who work within your genre or subject area. Similar organisations exist elsewhere. You could try a professional networking site such as LinkedIn, Upwork or Reedsy. Another option is to ask around. If you belong to a writing network or social media group, ask other writers who they worked with. A positive review or referral is always a good thing.

Once you've identified a few options, look at your chosen editors' websites and/or social media to see if they fit your requirements. Read their testimonials (obviously these will all be positive, but it gives you a view of how they work). Maybe ask them who they've worked with before and then approach that client and ask how the experience was. This is your creative work and your money and it's important to be sure it will be done correctly.

When you have a final list, contact these editors. Explain what you're looking for and ask for their rates. They are likely to ask for a sample of your writing so they can estimate how long the edit will take them and, therefore, give you as accurate a quote as possible (the more work the manuscript requires or the faster you need it completed, the more they will charge you). Choose the samples you send from different sections of the book. I have a tendency to edit the start of my books more heavily, so I also send material from further on as a contrast. Maybe send them sections with a lot of dialogue and others that are more description-based. The more accurate picture you can give them, the more realistic their quote will be. Don't forget, an editor may turn you down if your project doesn't suit them or if they are fully-booked.

You may decide to ask for a sample edit. Here you pay the editor to edit a section of the book so you can see how they work. You could send the same section to a few editors to compare the work they do. What feels right for you? Did they find the same errors? How did you feel about the way they communicated?

Don't just make a decision based on finances. Look at the quality of the editor's work and their suitability for your project. If you feel a particular editor is right for your book, then they may be the best choice even if they charge more money. Once you're happy, let your chosen editor know you would like to work with them and schedule a mutually convenient start date. They may be booked weeks in advance, so it's important to organise this early.

Resources

Grammarly: www.grammarly.com
Chicago referencing manual of style: www.
   chicagomanualofstyle.org
CIEP (formerly SfEP): www.ciep.uk
Reedsy: reedsy.com
Upwork: www.upwork.com

Illustrations

I know this section won't apply to everybody but, for those of you who are publishing illustrated books, I wanted to include it. Some of these points will also be helpful if you're illustrating your cover, so don't skip this chapter too hastily. In this section I will go over different illustrating options and tips for getting your artwork into your book.

Although the words in an illustrated book are important, the imagery is arguably even more so. Customers often pick up illustrated books because they are drawn to the artwork. Don't forget that if you're publishing a children's book, you want children to like the book, but also adults, since they're the ones actually buying it.

This is another area where you do a bodge job at your peril. If you require the services of a professional illustrator, you'll need to include this in your budget. Illustrating is expensive, and rightly so given the time and skill it takes. This can be frustrating when you have a beautiful story and you realise that it's no easy task to turn it into a physical book. However, if your budget is limited, there are options.

Do your research

As always, make sure you know what you want. Is your book a picture book aimed at younger readers? Are you looking for small vignettes in a middle-grade story? Do you want to include pretty drawings to augment a book for adults?

You should have an idea of the overall layout. You'll need to know how many illustrations you want and where they will be placed. Think about the layout of the text to make sure images will work around it. Children's picture books, typically, comprise twelve to fourteen double page spreads with single or multiple illustrations, and you may also want small design elements for preliminary pages. Be aware if you use a POD publishing company they will likely expect a blank page at the end of the book to add an identifying barcode (look at the last page of this book to see what I mean). If you don't include this in your formatting, they might add blank pages to make it work. Some companies require your book to be in page number multiples of four and, again, will add blank pages to make your book up to that number. Check the platform you are planning to use and any formatting requirements they have. This will help inform you on how many illustrations you want in your book.

Start by looking at books. Go to the bookshop, library or raid your own bookshelves. Look at similar books and see which ones appeal to you. Are the illustrations across double spreads? Are they on one page only? Are they small line drawings? Think about style and colour. Do you like bright colours, pastels or muted tones? Do you prefer hand-drawn images or digital art? What do the books you're attracted to have in common? What do books in your genre typically look like? Get a good idea of the kind of look you want your book to have and why.

When you're looking at books, consider size and think about whether you prefer portrait, landscape or square books. Be wary of landscape – it might limit your options as fewer landscape trim sizes are available through POD services. You will need to decide on the exact trim size of your book so that your illustrations are made to the right scale; having to fix them in the formatting stage is difficult, and you definitely don't want to have to start them all over again. Ensure that whatever trim size you go for has all the options you want enabled (certain ones may not be available for expanded distribution or particular binding options, for example).

Think about the text. Are you going to leave whole pages for it or do you need your illustrator to leave space within their illustrations? Will your text flow around the pictures? You may want your illustrator to format the book. If so, they will make sure the text works with the illustrations.

Start to build a mood board. This could be a physical cork board or a scrap book. Print out pictures that appeal to you and take cuttings from magazines. Or, easier and more shareable, make some boards on Pinterest. Look for book illustrations, but also images, colours and styles. On Pinterest you can add notes to explain to anybody you share the board with why you have chosen each pin.

By using this research you should have a better idea of what you want your book to look like when you begin to explore your options.

Illustrate it yourself

If you have the skills – go for it! However, I have learned that simply being able to draw does not qualify you to illustrate an entire book. But, if you are capable of producing suitable digital or physical art, there's no reason why you can't do it all. If it's good enough for Roger Hargreaves and Beatrix Potter, it's good enough for anyone!

If you're not sure, why not have a go so you can rule it out if it doesn't work? Consider asking friends (or people you trust to be honest with you) whether your work is professional enough (remember, some people will always say your work is good even if it's not). You could also take a course to improve your skills. Companies such as Teachable, Skillshare or Domestika offer online training that may give you help and inspiration. There are also many YouTube tutorials on all different kinds of art and media.

Plan the work out according to your research. Invest in good quality materials if you are doing the work by hand. Use appropriate software (you may have to pay for this) if you're doing the work digitally. If you are planning to use stock artwork or online tools, check they are licensed for commercial use (more on this later).

Ask a friend

If you have an amazing, generous, artistic friend or relative – ask them. This is the route I took with my second book and, for us, it worked well. Asking someone you know can be advantageous in that they are someone you trust and will probably enjoy working with. It also may allow you to have more flexible agreements than working with a professional.

Be aware that you cannot ask them to do this for free – illustrating a book is a huge task that may well take a lot longer than writing the words did. Research professional illustrating before you approach them so that you are fully aware of the scale of the favour you're asking.

A friend may be more willing than a professional to work for a royalty share or a payment plan. However, if you're paying them up front, make sure you negotiate a fair price. The same goes for any royalties you will pay them. Research standard arrangements and be fair.

Remember these things can break a friendship. What if you hate their artwork? What if they don't deliver? What if you never make any profit and they receive no royalties? Be honest with each other to manage expectations. It would also be advisable to draw up a legal agreement to protect the final product and your relationship. Decide between you when the work will be complete, how they will be paid and what rights you both have over the work. The clearer you are at the start, the better you protect yourself, your friendship and the book.

Hire an illustrator

Illustrating is time-consuming, so expect to pay well for it. If you don't, you may well get what you pay for. Typically, you can pay £1500–£3000 for a children's picture book but prices vary. Illustrators that are just starting out may work for less. Digital artwork might be cheaper (although often it isn't – you are paying for skill, experience and time, not materials). Having more or less artwork will also change pricing, which is why it's important to know what you want. Perhaps you can pull the illustrations into budget by having them on one page only. Your vision of three illustrations on each spread may be out of reach. Or maybe your budget will allow you to have it all! Know what you have to spend and what you hope to get for that money before you start approaching freelancers.

Many illustrators are paid a one-off fee for their work. Others may also wish for royalties once the book is profitable. These are considerations you will have to think about.

Finding an illustrator, in my experience, can be difficult. Many work for agencies and most don't put their prices on their websites. This means you have to send queries to several illustrators, rather than simply browsing the internet. Unfortunately, some simply won't work with self-published authors. It can feel overwhelming.

You might want to try Upwork, Reedsy or Fiverr. You can also use children's independent publishing Facebook groups to find illustrators. You could even scroll through Instagram for suitable artists. Again, always be wary of anyone you find online and be careful to check that they will deliver.

If you find someone online that you like, within your price bracket, and you are confident they will produce the work well and on time, send them a query. You will need to be clear about what you want them to produce and check if the work will be exclusive to you. If they are sharing it in their portfolios, think about whether you are happy with that. Have a signed agreement between you that lays out the rights of the artwork and the arrangements for paying the illustrator. Remember, this illustrator's name is going to be on the front of your book and their pictures will shape your story. Be sure that you have chosen the right person.

Once you have made your decision, contact them to make arrangements. You will need to communicate with them all of the information you gathered during your research; the trim size, how many images you require and what you're looking for stylistically. They should send you sketches of the work before it's finalised. If you aren't happy – tell them! You certainly don't want to be asking for changes to the finished artwork. Once all the work is complete (and you've paid them) they will send it to you in the format agreed (physical or digital).

How to work with physical artwork

If you have completed artwork yourself, or your illustrator has sent you the originals, you will need to convert this into a digital format to work with when you are formatting.

There are two ways to go about this. Some people take quality photographs of the artwork. If you have a good camera, and suitable lighting, this may work for you. The other option is scanning. Generally, household scanners are not up to the job. Local reprographics companies should be able to scan the images for you at a reasonable price. If they do this, have a look at the images on the screen to check you're happy with the quality and colours before they scan all of the artwork. A word from experience – these machines tend to wash out light colours.

Formatting

Since the sections on formatting later will focus on text, I will take a moment to briefly talk about the specifics on how to format illustrated books.

Once you have the files, you're ready to start manipulating the images. Some people like to use Photoshop. This allows you to 'fix' any issues or adjust colours if necessary. Others find it difficult to use, but there are lots of online tutorials to help. Photoshop gives you tools to edit photographs or images to make something beautiful and unique. It costs £19.97 a month on an annual plan or £30.34 on a monthly plan, although it is possible to get one month's free trial. There are free alternatives (such as Gimp) and many online tutorials on how to use them too.

You can format your book in InDesign, which costs the same as Photoshop (you can also get a package for all Adobe apps) You can also use Pages or Word. Another option is Canva but you can't view your pages as a spread, which may make things more challenging, depending on the nature of your book.

Firstly, set your document size to your chosen trim size. You will need to include bleed margins to avoid the risk of having white line around your images when the pages are cut. Check with the publishing platform you're using what margins they expect, but, in general, it's about 3mm added on each outside edge of the page (not the inside gutter). If you use a word processor, make sure your document is set as a page layout so you can layer the text and images without it impacting other pages. Set it to view as a double page spread if possible. Again, there are tutorials on YouTube on how to do this if you get stuck.

Drop in your pictures and text and format them how you wish. Remember that anything in the gutter (the inner margin or middle of the book) may be hard to see, particularly in perfect bound books.

Your full book can then be exported as a PDF ready to be uploaded. Certain companies (particularly Ingram Spark) require CMYK settings on their PDFs which aren't compatible with exports from Pages or Word (at the time of writing). The CMYK colour mode is preferable for print while RGB is for viewing on screen, otherwise the colours may not look right. The Adobe programs can export your files with this setting. If you need to covert your file, use Photoshop or a similar program to change the parameters of the PDF and rebuild it.

Resources

Pinterest: www.pinterest.co.uk
Teachable: teachable.com
Domestika: www.domestika.org
Skillshare: skillshare.com
Photoshop: www.photoshop.com/en
Gimp: www.gimp.org
InDesign: www.adobe.com
Canva: www.canva.com
YouTube: www.youtube.com

Cover Design

Cover design is one of my favourite parts of publishing. There's something special about seeing the artwork that will wrap around your book; it's like the moment a bride puts on her jewellery and veil.

Cover design is not something that should be rushed or skimped on. A good cover can make a book and help to sell it. You want your artwork to attract customers: to make them click on your book when browsing online; to pick it up in a shop; or to stop scrolling on Instagram. A poorly finished or unattractive cover is going to make your book look unprofessional and the job of marketing considerably harder.

Do your research

It's best to start out by getting an idea of what you want in a cover. Browse libraries, bookshops and your own shelves. See what kind of covers jump out at you. Have a look at books in the same genres as yours and study their design. Are you going to follow a similar style so your book is clearly part of the family, or are you looking to create something a bit different to stand out?

Another good way to research is on Pinterest. Again, search for book covers and pin any that interest you, whether within your genre or otherwise. I also like to pin artwork, photography and anything I find inspiring when thinking of my book. These Pinterest boards help to build up an idea of the kind of imagery you're looking for.

The next thing to research is trim size. As discussed in the illustration chapter, you'll need to choose a suitable size for your book. There are industry standards for particular types of books but, as always, there's some variability. Look at different books in your genre and see what sizes you like. Also check what's available through the platforms you're using (and whether those sizes are enabled for expanded distribution and the print options you want).

Think about what formats you're going to publish in. If you are having multiple formats, you might need multiple cover designs. Ebooks and audiobooks require only a front page image in a certain size (check specifications). Print will require a full wrap, where the back cover and spine are included. To find out the specifications of the spine allowance for your book you will need to know how many pages it comprises and the type of paper you are going to use.

The spine width and format specifications may vary by platform. So, if you're using more than one platform or printer for a single format, there could be small differences meaning you may require more than one cover for the same format. For instance, if you are using KDP and Ingram Spark to publish your paperback, you might need slightly different versions of the cover to fit their requirements (however they will carry the same ISBN because they are the same format). It's important to carefully check the cover guidelines for the platforms you're using. You need to know their specific requirements in terms of spine allowance, bleed margins, barcode placement and any other relevant information.

If you're going to put a price on the back cover of your print edition, you should research suitable pricing at this point. You can use royalty calculators on the platforms you intend to use to help you make a decision. If you're self-distributing a bulk printed book, you will need to research the fees charged by the outlets you wish to sell through. If the price is printed on the cover, it's harder to change at a later date.

Blurb

If you haven't already done so, you should now write a blurb for the back cover of your print editions. Of course, this will also appear on online listings. Think about how to make your book sound as exciting and appealing to the reader as possible so they absolutely have to buy it. You're aiming at about 100-150 words (less for children's books). Have a look at blurbs from similar books for ideas on how to write yours. You should tell the reader everything they need to know about the book as simply and succinctly as possible, without giving away too much. Even in an autobiography or memoir, this should be written in third person (which is really weird when you're writing it yourself). If you're not sure, ask beta readers to have a look at what you've written and give you their opinion. It is advisable to ask your editor to look over the final version of the blurb to ensure it's error-free.

Illustrated books

If your book is illustrated, the cover will form part of the illustrator's work, whether you're completing that yourself or otherwise. Obviously, the cover must reflect the style of the interior pages. If you're doing your own illustrating, you should consider the cover's design. If you're working with an illustrator, ask them if you need additional cover work. Or, if you prefer, you could repeat an interior illustration.

Design it yourself

If you're trying to limit expenditure, and you have the relevant skills, why not design the cover yourself? If you're a good graphic designer, artist or photographer, you may be able to translate those skills into cover design. If you have the ability, give it a try. BUT – and it's a big but – don't do it if it's not within your skill set. Be realistic about whether the artwork looks professional enough and whether it's comparable to industry standards. Ask your beta readers for critique.

When you set your budget, cover design may be something that you have to pay for – it's just part of the business. However, if you have the ability to do this yourself, it can help to substantially reduce costs.

Creating images

It is possible to create your own image for your cover, whether you paint it, photograph it or create something digitally. Have a look back at the illustration section for ideas and tips on producing your own artwork. One option is to use stock images from Shutterstock or similar sites and manipulate them. Be absolutely sure you're able to use these images and pay for their usage if you need to. You may need to credit the source. You don't want to infringe licensing regulations.

If you have physical artwork, it will need to be photographed or scanned (again, see the illustration section). Once you have your cover image in a digital format, you are ready to piece it together with the spine and back cover, as well as manipulating it for ebook and audiobook covers.

Adobe Photoshop

Photoshop is a standard tool in graphic design and it can be used it to create attractive cover artwork. As previously mentioned, it costs £19.97 a month on an annual plan or £30.34 on a monthly plan (they also offer a free trial). Some people find it tricky to use. However, if you are familiar with Photoshop, or consult online tutorials, you can manipulate images to create a professional looking cover, including text and formatting. InDesign is also a good tool for formatting a full wrap. It's available individually at the prices above or can be bought in a bundle with other Adobe apps.

Canva

Canva is a useful tool for piecing your cover together. Certain 'premium' elements and fonts have associated costs, and you can pay monthly for added features, but a great deal is available for free.

Check the size specifications for your book and set your file up accordingly. I like to download templates from the POD or printing companies and build my artwork on top of them so I can view guidelines when I need to. You simply drop in images and text and adjust them as you wish.

You can create your cover using one of the template designs. Just be wary of it being obviously made this way; a lot of people use Canva so it will be easily spotted that you've taken an easy route to create your cover. You will need to significantly customise the template to make sure it's unique.

As a side note, Canva is your friend for creating marketing artwork. I use it for creating all kinds of media from Instagram posts to flyers. For print you may prefer to use a program that exports to CMYK or use a file converter.

Kindle Cover Creator

If you're using KDP to publish your book, you can use Kindle Cover Creator for free. There are layout templates to help you to place the different elements. You have a choice of using your own images or selecting from their gallery. You then overlay text for your title, name and blurb. Again, using stock designs may mark your book as amateurish so use them wisely.

Like all KDP tools, be aware that you cannot use your files outside of their ecosystem.

Ask a friend

As with illustrating, you could ask a talented friend if they would be willing to help you. Again, don't expect them to do it for free. This arrangement has the advantage of working with a person you know and trust.

If you decide to go down this route, discuss who owns the art copyright and what can be done with it. Are they allowed to publicise it? If so, when? Can they use it for other projects? Can you? Or is it exclusive to the book? It would be sensible to draw up an agreement between you in order to protect your relationship and the creative work.

Hire a designer

You may decide the way forward is to hire a designer. Some designers are solo freelancers, while others are part of a larger company (such as Damonza). Some are genre specific and others are more general. The designer that suits you will depend on your taste and budget.

Often designers provide packages that include a combination of print and ebook covers along with mockups to use in your marketing. They may also offer interior formatting and often it doesn't cost much more. You may decide to add extras such as promotional items or additional formats. Have a look at what different designers offer and see if they have a package to suit you. Depending on what you want (how many formats, number of changes allowed, etc.), you are looking to spend in the region of £300-600.

Finding a designer

Word of mouth is a good way to find a designer; ask other self-published and indie authors who they worked with if you like the look of their books. An internet search can also be helpful. As before, you could try sites such as Reedsy, Upwork or Fiverr. It is also worth checking curated lists from professional bodies or writing associations.

As always, make sure you do your homework on anybody you find online. You don't want to pay for a cover that looks nothing like you expected, or one that never materialises. Even worse, one that's used copyrighted imagery. Check who the designer has worked with before and ensure they produce the kind of artwork you're looking for. Refer back to your research and check they fit your requirements. You should also check they are familiar with formatting for the platforms or printer you will be using and so will be comfortable with the specifics.

Whoever you use, you want to be sure they will still be around if you want to work with them in the future. If you wish to add a format, make small changes or add promotional items, you want to do so using the same artwork and branding. If your book is part of a series, you might want to use the same designer for future books so that they tie in. Look at how long a designer has been in the industry, if they seem to be reliable and whether they will be easily contactable in the future.

Working with a designer

Send a query to the designer or designers you have selected to see if they can work on the project. Establish their schedule (for some you might have to wait a long time) and see if it fits into your timeline. Ensure they can fulfil your design requirements and fit your budget.

You should then provide your chosen designer with all the necessary information about what you're looking for. Send them your title, blurb, trim size, number of pages, ISBNs, formats, platforms and prices. If you have a publishing company name and logo, send that too. You might also want them to include websites or social media icons. Describe what kind of imagery you're looking for and link them to any Pinterest boards you've created. Make sure you also mention anything you specifically don't want. The more you can tell them, the more likely they are to get it right.

The designer is likely to send you a few concepts. Hopefully, if you've sent them enough information, you'll like at least one of them. If you're struggling to choose your favourite, try testing it out on other people and ask for their feedback. If you don't like any of your designer's initial ideas, politely explain what you were hoping to see and ask them to have another go. Once you have a concept you're happy with, ask them to proceed. They will add details and embellishments and come back to you with a finalised design. You should still be able to ask for any final tweaks before signing off on it.

Resources

Pinterest: www.pinterest.co.uk
Shutterstock: www.shutterstock.com
Canva: www.canva.com
Photoshop: www.photoshop.com/en
Kindle Cover Creator: kdp.amazon.com/en_US/help/topic/G201113520
Fiverr: www.fiverr.com
Upwork: www.upwork.com
Reedsy: reedsy.com
Damonza: damonza.com

Formatting an ebook

So now your content is beautifully edited and you have eye-catching artwork, I'm going to go through how to turn this into the final product. In the next few sections we'll cover ebooks.

Since ebooks took off over the last twenty years or so (although they've been around longer!) they have become extremely important to the book industry, and particularly to self-published authors. Ebooks are arguably easy to produce and distribute online, with just your home computer and internet access, and there's no need to hold physical copies. They can also confer a high royalty rate.

It's definitely worthwhile having an ebook version of your book, not only to sell but also to offer as promotional copies.

Do your research

Decide what ebook publishing platforms you wish to use. This may have a bearing on formatting. See what different companies have to offer and what you think might work for your book (more information on this in the next chapter).

Ebooks are usually EPUB files, so you'll have to change your working document (doc, docx, pages, etc.) to a suitable file type. Also check any other file specifications before you get started – you don't want to put in all the work and discover your files are useless.

Have a think about what sections of your book you would like to include in your ebook; it may be different to your print edition. You would generally not include an index (people can search the text). Your copyright page may also look a little different.

Hire a professional

As with all other stages, you can hire a professional. If it's within budget and you feel you do not have the skills to format the files yourself, then consider this option. You may have invested in a cover design package that included ebook file creation. If you work with someone for this job, let them know what platforms you are using so they can format the files appropriately.

Bear in mind that you may have limited revisions with someone who formats the book for you, and they may charge you. You also won't have the working files should you need to make changes in the future – this is mainly only an issue if the company or person who formatted them is no longer in business.

Do it yourself

By creating the ebook yourself you keep control of the files and can make small tweaks if you need to (maybe someone spots an errant typo, or perhaps a piece of information you referenced has changed). It's not especially tricky to do and there are blogs and video tutorials that explain different aspects of creating your files.

There are *loads* of programs you can use to do this. Each has pros and cons. I will go through the better known ones, but do your research and find what works for you. Some are paid programs and others are free, so there is a budgetary consideration. The decision will also depend on the look you're going for, the operating system you use and your level of technological ability.

Fonts

Ebooks are typically formatted using standard fonts so users are able to change the style or size. If you want to use a specific font for style reasons, you will need to embed it.

Any fonts you use need to be licensed for commercial use, and there is an extra licensing level for ebooks. So, you need to find open source fonts or pay for licences (which can be expensive). Personally, I use Font Squirrel which has a clear indicator of the licensing level of each font and has the ability to sort by licence types, making it easy to check before you download whether you are allowed to use the fonts for ebooks.

SELF-PUBLISHING

Reflowable/fixed ebooks

If you want your book to adjust its layout depending on the device it's being read on, you need to ensure your files are 'reflowable' rather than having a fixed layout. It enables readers to change font sizes and easily highlight and search through the text. Images make reflowable books more complex, so if you want your artwork set in a particular way, a fixed layout will suit you better.

Links

In an ebook you have the option to add links to your website, books, social media, affiliate links...anything! If this suits you, add them in and don't forget to make sure they work. You could even make them trackable.

Page numbers

Remove your page numbers! Maybe this seems obvious, but it's something that some people forget. Ebooks don't have page numbers so they will just make your book look amateurish. Instead, your table of contents links to your text to allow readers to easily navigate your book.

Check your files

Often what you see on the page doesn't work perfectly. Make sure you preview your ebook through the platform you're using to ensure it looks as you expected. Then, if you spot anything that doesn't look quite right, you can go back to your document, tweak and re-export. You're likely to have to do this a few times, especially if this is the first time you have created ebook files.

Programs

Apple Pages/Microsoft Word

I'm a Mac user (much to my Apple-ambivalent husband's disgust). The word processor Apple Pages has now incorporated much of the functionality of the iBooks Author app (iBooks Author is no longer available to new users and isn't updated).

Pages can export files with reflowable or fixed attributes. Just paste your text, then choose your fonts and your formatting. If you do this by selecting styles for each element (titles, paragraphs, etc.), you don't have to spend tedious time selecting specific parts of your book. Once you've finished you simply export as an EPUB file.

You can use Microsoft Word similarly. However, you will require a clean version of your document that is free of any background code from formatting and editing. A good way to do this is to copy your book into Microsoft Notes, change it to plain text and paste it back into a fresh Word document. You shouldn't have headers, footers, custom margins or any unique page sizes. You want the plainest of documents. Again, set up your formatting in styles rather than tampering with the whole body of text. Have a check through and export the files once you're happy.

Vellum

Vellum produces beautiful looking ebooks, and you can try it out for free to see if it will work for you. However, if you want to actually use the file, you need to pay, and it doesn't come cheap at £199 for just the ebook version (although you can create unlimited future ebooks with it). Vellum is Mac only (and doesn't work on iPads). It's easy to use, simply adding your content to customisable templates. The aesthetics are good, and it includes a useful preview tool that allows you to see how your book looks on different readers.

Adobe InDesign

Adobe InDesign is a standard tool used by designers for creating print and digital media, and it can also be used for ebooks. It can be tricky to use if you're unfamiliar with Adobe programs, but there are online tutorials to help.

Once you have set up your document (you can format to the size of a standard e-reader if you wish), select digital publishing. You then copy across your content and manipulate it. InDesign also gives you the option of anchoring images in reflowable ebooks to help the layout look tidier. InDesign requires a monthly or yearly subscription, but has a lot of functionality.

Scrivener

Many writers use Scrivener for the actual writing process. It allows you to build your book in sections which are easily moved and adjusted. You can also view your outline, notes or research alongside your manuscript. It's then easy to create your book files directly from your working document. Once you're happy, you compile, set your styles, check through everything and save!

Scrivener has a one-time cost of £47. It's definitely not the most expensive program available, and worth the money if you find it a useful tool.

Reedsy Book Editor

Reedsy offers a free ebook creation tool from by the same people you may have used to find your freelancers. You paste your book into the editor, choose your styles and check it through. The templates are limited, but professional looking. Reedsy is different to previously mentioned tools in that it's website-based, so you will require an internet connection and be logged in to the website to use it.

Draft2Digital (D2D)

D2D have their own ebook creator which has some good templates. The tool is free, and, although created by a self-publishing platform, there is no requirement to only use it through them. Like Reedsy, this tool is web-based.

SELF-PUBLISHING

Kindle Create

Kindle's own tool, Kindle Create is also easy to use. You open your document within the tool and you are straight in to editing it. You then choose fonts, add drop caps and fix errors within the text.

You can only use the generated files for KDP, so if your intention is to publish wide, you will need to generate another file for other platforms, or skip Kindle Create altogether. If you are going exclusive through KDP, however, this tool works well.

Kindle Kids' Book Creator

If you're publishing a picture book, this is an easy-to-use tool. As with Kindle Create, you can only use your files for KDP. But, if that's what you plan to do, consider giving this a go.

To use, download the software which will guide you through the steps. You have the option of uploading your cover separately or including it as the first page of your interior file, which the program will automatically separate. You can choose to make your pages appear singly or in double page spreads, depending on the nature of your illustrations and layouts. You may choose to add text 'pop-ups' if your font size has now become hard to read; just select the area and add your text. When a user selects the area, the text will 'pop-up' larger for them to read. Once you're happy with your formatting, save the file ready to publish.

Resources

Font Squirrel: www.fontsquirrel.com
Scrivener: www.literatureandlatte.com
Vellum: vellum.pub
InDesign: www.adobe.com
Reedsy Book Editor: reedsy.com/write-a-book
Draft2Digital: www.draft2digital.com
Kindle Create: www.amazon.com/Kindle-Create/
  b?ie=UTF8&node=18292298011
Kindle Kids' Book Creator: kdp.amazon.com/en_US/how-
  to-publish-childrens-books

Publishing an ebook

In this section I will outline the different platforms you can use to publish your ebook and the basic information you need to know – it's beyond the scope of this book to give how-to guides for each platform. Nonetheless, there are many online tutorials if you find it tricky.

There is a lot to take in here; I know I found it overwhelming at the start. There are several different options depending on your vision for your book. Refer back to your plans and spend time researching the platforms that appeal to you. A path will become clear.

You should be uploading your book a good few weeks before the release date. This gives you time to fix any problems you encounter and allows for marketing. I personally feel six to eight weeks works well, but you can amend this to suit your marketing and release plans. Most sites enable you to set a pre-order sale period to direct people to buy your book in advance of its release.

Do your research

Pricing

You will need to consider pricing. Look at similar books and the price for the ebook editions. Look at other books in your genre as well as those of similar lengths and by a variety of authors. I like to compare traditionally published and indie books as well. You can change your pricing any time if you feel it's not suitable.

If your book is the first in a series, you might consider pricing it low (or for free) when the rest of the series comes out, in order to generate readers' interest. If you're going to use subscription based models (whether Kindle Unlimited or otherwise), you will also need to find out how they work and how that impacts the prices you set.

Exclusive vs wide

One thing to consider is your approach to platform. Are you going to make your book available exclusively to Amazon or will you publish wide across multiple platforms?

Amazon has a huge market share when it comes to ebooks. Publishing direct with KDP and signing up to their exclusivity program, KDP Select, allows you to offer your books 'for free' to Kindle Unlimited members for a per-page royalty. This may give you access to an audience who are willing to flick through books to try them since they aren't paying per book. It also enables you to run free promotional periods which may be helpful in garnering reviews. However, signing up to this makes you exclusive to KDP and unable to publish or distribute your ebook anywhere else (including free promotional copies). Once signed up, you remain in the program for 90 days.

Publishing wide, across other platforms, gives you access to readers outside of the Amazon market. This gives you access to a wider readership, including those using subscription and library services. However, it excludes you from being part of KDP Select and, therefore, accessing KU subscribers.

If you choose to publish wide, you can go directly to the various platforms, which gives you the advantage of specifically controlling your pricing and metadata. Or, you can use aggregator sites such as Draft2Digital or Smashwords who will distribute your book to multiple platforms with you only needing to upload once. Below is a list of some of the major players.

Ebook vendors:
Kindle
Kobo
Barnes and Noble (formerly Nook) Press
Apple Books
Google Play Books

SELF-PUBLISHING

Aggregators:
Draft2Digital
Smashwords
Ingram Spark
Publish Drive
StreetLib

If you're using an aggregator, you should check who they distribute to. If they don't work with a particular platform that is important to you, consider going direct. Aggregators take a percentage royalty on top of the retailers, which reduces your royalties. However, it makes the job quicker!

Your decision will depend on how you feel about distribution. There's also no harm in experimenting and seeing what works best for you. You can start off with Kindle Select and go wide after 90 days. Or publish wide and then pull your book and try just selling through Amazon.

Set up your book

To publish through any of these companies you will need your book cover saved as a JPG, PNG or TIFF and your interior files in an EPUB format as discussed in the formatting section. Always check the specific requirements of your platform.

None of the sites are particularly hard to use. You simply fill in the information, upload your files and you're ready to go. If you reach a section you're not sure about, or need to research, save what you have completed so far and go back to it another time. There is usually guidance on the sites about how to fill in all the information; remember, they're used to newbies. Of course, until you press 'publish', you can alter things as much as you need in order get it all right.

The following are the basic fields you should expect to fill in:

Title/Subtitle

This is self-explanatory! But if you have a subtitle there may or may not be a box for it. If there isn't, just separate it from the main title with a colon. If you don't have a subtitle, leave this section blank.

Contributors

Here you add in your author name and anyone else who should be listed on the cover, such as your illustrator.

ISBN

Depending on your publishing plans you may not need an ISBN - some sites just use an identifier. Either give your ISBN, or select that you wish to be supplied with one or won't be using one (as appropriate). If you have your own, you will need to give your publisher name, which is the name you used when you bought your ISBNs.

SELF-PUBLISHING

Description

Put your blurb in here! Sometimes you are also asked for a shortened description, so you might need to come up with an abridged version. You may be able to add reader quotes, reviews, prizes or anything else relevant to marketing the book if you choose to.

Keywords

You will generally be asked to come up with keywords and/ or categories to help list your book appropriately. These will help with searchability, so be creative! Think of search terms related to the subject of the book.

For categories, you will usually have to choose from a menu. If you are asked for a BISAC code and the platform doesn't give you an easily navigable menu, go to the BISAC website and search for suitable categories that you can go back and add.

Age range

Certain sites may ask you to add an appropriate age range, particularly for children's books. If you're not sure, see how other similar books are categorised online.

Digital Rights Management

Enabling DRM, where you're able, gives a layer of protection to stop piracy, by preventing people from being able to share your book. On the flip side, this may limit readers sharing your book between their own devices. It's up to you if you want to enable this or not.

Publication date

Put in the date you wish your book to be released. You can set this in advance and your book will start collecting pre-sales. The customers will receive the book when it's released.

Upload your files

It's possible to experience file issues at this point. The platforms have verifiers that can throw up all sorts of issues you didn't expect – particularly if there are complex elements in your book such as tables, images or references. Different platforms may have problems with different parts. If you find this happens to you, you should get an idea of what the issue is from the error message, but if not, contact the company and ask for their support. They can usually advise you how to fix the problem. If you used a formatter, they might also be able to help.

Once everything is set up and ready to go you will usually be given an opportunity to view your book and check it looks right. Read through carefully and check it all looks as you expected it to. If anything has gone wrong, you are still able to go back to the files, fix any issues and re-upload.

SELF-PUBLISHING

Set your pricing

The last section is usually pricing. You will probably find the website automatically populates prices from other territories once you have added your price in dollars. I, personally, try a few different numbers and look at the royalties to help me decide whether I'm happy with my pricing. You should then go through all the territories and change the prices to commonly used numbers (ending in .99 or .49 rather than random numbers).

If you're uploading to a site that distributes to libraries (such as Draft2Digital), you will have to select a higher price for these institutions. This is standard since they only pay once but their customers will view the book multiple times. The site should recommend suitable prices based on the pricing you have set for direct customers.

* * *

Once you're happy, hit 'publish'. You will probably find there is approval time, so you may have to wait a day or two before your book starts popping up online (best not to upload on your publication day...)

Congratulations on a big step towards publishing your book!

Resources

KDP: kdp.amazon.com
Nook: press.barnesandnoble.com
Kobo: www.kobo.com/us/en/p/writinglife
Apple Books: authors.apple.com/epub-upload
Google Play: play.google.com/books/publish/u/0/
Publish Drive: www.publishdrive.com
Smashwords: www.smashwords.com
Draft2Digital: www.draft2digital.com
Ingram Spark: www.ingramspark.com
BISAC Codes: bisg.org/page/bisacedition

Formatting for Print

It's now relatively easy to produce a book in print with the tools you have at home. Of course, you may decide you want to publish in ebook only, and that's absolutely fine if that suits your goals. However, some readers only read print and you would be missing out this section of the market. There's something special about a physical copy of a book – and now we have POD you can access this option without storing lots of copies. Having print editions also makes it easier to work with brick-and-mortar stores and libraries. They are good props for your social media (print books are beautiful, after all) and you can even give them away as prizes. It also enables you to run selling and signing events – you can't sign an ebook.

There are now more options for POD — paperbacks, hardbacks and large print. If you use bulk printing, you have even more options and can even have board books. If you are hoping to have multiple print formats, you will require multiple cover and interior files (unless they have the same attributes). You can make your ebook and print copies stylistically similar, although print gives you scope to be more creative.

As with previous chapters, I will run through your options. You may need to format your interior files before your cover so you know how many pages your book comprises, but you will require both, obviously, to progress through to publishing.

As with cover design, you should have already researched the platform you wish to publish through in order to know your trim sizes and any other file requirements. Unlike ebooks, there isn't one simple trim size, so you will have to set these up yourself.

Hire a professional

As with ebooks, your interior formatting may be part of your cover design package. Or, it can be something you individually outsource. Formatting for print can be a little more involved than for ebook, but is still completely achievable yourself.

If you don't feel able to format the book, paying a professional can be really helpful. Remember to inform whoever is formatting your book if you are looking for anything specific with the design aspects of your interior files and advise them on your trim size and intended publishing platform. Do remember that, as with ebooks, it gives you limited access to files if you need to make alterations and you might have to pay for future changes should you find any errors.

Do it yourself

As for ebooks, doing your own formatting is possible with a laptop at home. You will need to produce a PDF file to upload to your self-publishing platform. As always, if you're not happy, you can go back to your original files and change them and, again, there are many tutorials online.

Design considerations

You will need an idea of what kind of look you're going for. Have a look at how other books are formatted and see what you are drawn to. Some have elaborate designs at the start of chapters and interesting fonts on titles. You can incorporate drawings and drop caps, or have stylistic breaks between chapters. Have a think about what you want. To an extent, it will also depend on your genre.

Before you start formatting, check any file submission guides for your platform or printer. You want to make sure your formatting is compliant so you don't have to spend extra time making amendments later.

Choose fonts that are easy to read (especially for the main text), and consider sticking to those that are commonly used. They also need to be enabled for commercial use as discussed in the section on formatting for ebooks. Again, Font Squirrel is a useful website. Ideally, a serif font in 12 point size will work well for the body of the text – keep it simple!

There are one or two standard considerations for formatting. There is no longer a double space after a full stop. Think about it this way, you're saving on the print cost for all those extra spaces – it probably amounts to a few pages! If you've used double spaces, don't worry; it's not necessary to edit each one individually. Do a document search for the double spaces and 'replace all' with a single space. Don't leave lines after paragraphs unless it's a section break. The first line of the first paragraph in a chapter or section should not be indented. Justify your text so it's aligned on the left and the spacing is adjusted to enable the lines to reach the right margin (with no hyphenation).

Consider how you want to set out headers and footers – where do you want page numbers and do you want to have the book title, your name or chapter headings in the header? Odd page numbers should appear on the right. Blank pages should not have numbers on. Bear in mind that your book will be viewed as spreads and set the pages as facing accordingly – if your elements are set to one side of the page, they should mirror on the facing pages (so, for example, if your numbering is on the outside edge, it will be on the left on even pages and the right on odd pages).

You will need to set up your page margins. Make sure they are not too large or small and the text is correctly placed on the page (it will look off-centre once you have allowed for the gutter). Consider measuring a few books to see what margins are commonly used and which look pleasing to you.

Look out for widow or orphan lines that appear as a result of formatting. This is where a line or a word hangs over onto the next page or at the end of a paragraph. It makes the book look messy and can make things confusing for the reader. You may be able to pull these back by adjusting letter spacing on other lines.

Don't forget to include a title page and copyright page at the start of the book. You can have a look at other books for examples of the wording used. You may also wish to add a contents page, particularly for non-fiction. This can be easily generated from the styles in the document when you are formatting. You might want to include an author bio and acknowledgements (thanking those who have helped you with your book). Again, looking at other books can give you an idea of how other people have phrased and laid out these sections. Finally, think about whether you need to add any blank pages to break up the content.

For POD platforms you usually have to leave the last page blank so they can add their own printing barcode (see the last page of this book for an example). If you don't, they will add extra pages so there is a blank page — check the file submission guides. Also, see if the page numbers need to be in a set multiple (sometimes four), since some platforms will add extra pages if your book does not conform to this.

SELF-PUBLISHING

Programs

Apple Pages/Microsoft Word

Again these word processors can be used for formatting and they do a perfectly adequate job. Start out by setting up the page size you want. If your book includes bleed margins, you will have to include them in your document size. Next, set up your margins, headers and footers. Then paste in your text and start formatting it as you wish. Once you're done, export as a PDF.

Remember to ensure your blank pages are truly blank. If you include blank pages, you will need to set them as the first page of a section. This allows you to choose different formatting for your 'first page' so it remains free of numbers, headings and footers.

There are limitations to using a word processor for formatting. If you are producing a PDF for a children's book, or with colour images using a word processor, the RGB settings aren't agreeable for certain platforms and don't produce accurate colours in print. It is possible to covert the images using Photoshop or similar and rebuild the PDF with CMYK settings.

InDesign

InDesign is a standard tool used by professional book designers. You need to set up your document properties and select facing pages. Create text boxes and allow them to flow so when you paste in your text it will fill subsequent pages. Set up your styles and parent pages, format as you wish and export. As mentioned in ebook formatting, InDesign produces lovely files, but it does incur a cost and can tricky to use.

Scrivener

Scrivener is a good tool for producing print books, especially if you're already using it for your writing. Add folders with any extra front and end matter (and any blank pages) so you can add those when you compile the book. Edit your page settings to the trim sizes and add all the settings for headers, footers and fonts. Once this is complete, compile your book and save as a PDF. Check it over to make sure everything looks as you'd hoped.

The ability to simply choose your settings and compile the book makes Scrivener an easy to use formatting tool, although not free.

Vellum

You can set up your print edition in Vellum and apply certain attractive preset styles to your book. Rather than having to create the styles for yourself you can simply select and customise which is user-friendly and aesthetically pleasing. For print, Vellum is more expensive, at £249.99 compared to £199.99 for just the ebook version. However, once again, you are able to set the book up first to see if it works before paying.

Draft2Digital (D2D)

D2D also has a layout tool for print. You simply upload your document, then choose your heading formats and trim size. They are in the beta phase of rolling out their own print distribution service but, as with ebook, you can use the print files anywhere you wish. They are not exclusive (especially since D2D doesn't have a print service at present). If you've used D2D to format your ebook, you can tie in the print copy by using their conversion tool for print.

Reedsy

As for ebooks, you can use Reedsy, and the process is much the same. Again, it's web-based only, but still has some useful formats.

* * *

Don't forget to proofread your final files (or use a professional proofreader). Sometimes a perfectly produced manuscript can suddenly acquire new issues after formatting such as duplicated sections, orphan/ widow lines, incorrect fonts or weird page numbering. This is also a last check for any spelling and grammar issues so take your time. I like to print out these final files and give them a last critical look with my red pen in hand before I upload them.

Resources

Damonza: damonza.com
Scrivener: www.literatureandlatte.com
InDesign: www.adobe.com
Vellum: vellum.pub
Draft2Digital: www.draft2digital.com
Reedsy: reedsy.com

Publishing in Print

There's something special about a physical book. Ebooks are brilliant, but holding your book in your hands, flicking through the pages and sniffing the unique scent of newly printed paper...it's wonderful.

Just like publishing ebooks, there are several different options to explore. I found it useful to see what other independent authors had done and why they had made those decisions. It helped me to weigh up the best options for my book. In particular, YouTube can be a great resource for this and there is a large community of 'AuthorTubers' making content about how they've navigated their way through the decision-making process.

While some of you may decide you don't wish to print physical copies of your book, it's now an achievable option for independently publishing authors. It is slightly more involved, but anyone with a laptop can do it. Many independent authors use POD, but others find bulk printing advantageous so I will cover both in this chapter.

Print on demand

There was a time when publishing in print meant buying piles of books, storing them in your garage and hoping for the best. The advent of the ebook gave a wonderful alternative, but POD has evolved the industry even more. It's not the only option, but it is very popular.

POD services will do exactly that – print a book and distribute it when someone orders it. You can also order author copies to sell yourself, but if you prefer everything to be handled by your POD company then that is an option. They will print, package and ship your book without you lifting a finger – wonderful! It's great in terms of storage and wastage, but the books do cost significantly more per copy than if you ordered a bulk print run. In addition, you might find there are limitations in terms of trim sizes, paper stocks and so on. Some options simply aren't possible (such as thicker paper, board books, or those with design elements such as glitter, embossing or fold-out sections) but, in general, POD can suit many requirements.

There are a few companies that offer POD services, and I will run through how they vary to enable you to make a decision on what suits you and your book. I will then go through additional tips for uploading to these platforms.

KDP

As discussed for ebooks, KDP is part of Amazon. So, therefore, it's set up to function well through their site.

The book set-up is simple, and similar to that for the ebook. You can also tie your formats together in your author dashboard.

KDP offer great royalties on books sold through Amazon. However, their expanded distribution offers low royalties (due to an enforced 55% wholesale discount), and I have found issues with getting brick-and-mortar stores to stock my books if they are published through KDP.

If you are primarily interested in selling through Amazon and you want a straightforward service, KDP may suit your requirements but, if you want your books to be distributed anywhere else, this may not be the best choice. However, you have the option to use KDP in conjunction with another company, provided you don't tick the 'expanded distribution' box.

Additionally, KDP do not currently offer a presale period for print books, so if you were hoping to generate pre-sales you may have to consider using them along with another platform or taking advance sales on your website ahead of the release date.

Ingram Spark

Ingram Spark is part of the Ingram Content Group, they are the self-publishing arm of the distribution and printing company. For that reason, they were initially more geared up for specialists in the industry and so were more complex for a beginner to use. Ingram Spark had a reputation for being user unfriendly, however, recent improvements to their site has made it much easier to navigate, and I think it's now comparable to other companies. Ingram Spark has also added the option of a free ISBN for US authors.

Ingram Spark's big selling point is its expanded distribution. It's partnered with a number of companies that make this easy and it also allows you to set your own wholesale discount between 30 and 55%. This makes expanded distribution a more viable option for self-published authors, when you take into account higher printing costs. You can keep your pricing competitive while being able to distribute widely.

It's worth pointing out that the lower you set your wholesale discount, the less attractive the book becomes to small brick-and-mortar stores. Larger organisations may be comfortable, but smaller shops are less able to buy books with a small wholesale discount. You might like to check if any of the retailers you are hoping to work with have limitations.

Ingram Spark charges a fee for their service, and you have to pay for any revisions so it's important to get your files right before you publish and pay. Do check for free codes though – they're available if you join organisations such as the Alliance of Independent Authors (ALLi).

Ingram Spark doesn't offer as good a royalty rate through Amazon as KDP, but again you can use the companies in conjunction. If you do, you may find that if Ingram Spark ships their books to the Amazon warehouse before KDP has started producing them (for example, if you are using Ingram Spark during your presale phase). Amazon will sell off the

Ingram Spark copies before printing their own. So, don't panic if you don't see any sales for a while.

Barnes and Noble Press

Formerly Nook Press, Barnes and Noble Press relaunched in 2018. Obviously, using this platform gives you easy access to Barnes and Noble online and Nook readers, with incentives of more visibility if you sell more books. However, they do not offer the option for a wholesale discount and, therefore, your books will not sell elsewhere.

Barnes and Noble offer free ISBNs or will use ones you have bought elsewhere. They do not charge a fee to use the service and offer good royalty rates.

They will only ship personal copies (if you wish to sell them yourself) within the US. When combined with exclusivity to their own stores, this makes them difficult to use outside of America.

Lulu Press

Lulu have a fairly simple to use platform and, reportedly, have good print quality. They are first and foremost a printer, so great if you just want a couple of copies of your book for your family and friends. You also receive a good royalty on books sold on their website.

Lulu have high printing costs and set large wholesaler discounts. This means having to set a higher cost to customers in order to make royalties, making it hard to price your book competitively.

Blurb

Blurb's strength is in visual books with great quality and creation for photo books or magazines. They distribute through Ingram Spark so you have access to their outlets and the option to set your own discounts to give you more pricing flexibility. If you are creating an artistic or highly visual book, Blurb might work for you.

Set up your book

As with publishing your ebook, you now need to fill in all of the fields on your chosen publishing platform. There will be a crossover so see the chapter on publishing an ebook. However, there are a few extra elements.

Printing options

There will be sections where you select your chosen print options. This is likely to be in the form of tick boxes where you choose various options. There is usually information to help you. If you have left plenty of time, you will be able to order a proof copy and then go back to make alterations if it doesn't look quite right (if you use Ingram Spark where certain revisions incur a fee).

You will need to select a binding type. Paperback books may be available perfect bound (pages glued to spine) or saddle bound (book stapled through the middle). Hardcover books are generally available cloth bound or case laminate (where the cover is printed with your cover design) and may come with or without a dust jacket.

You can usually choose white or cream paper. White paper looks good and ages well. Cream may be more reader-friendly due to the reduced contrast, particularly for those with dyslexia. You might also be able to select different paper weights or printing qualities. There are resources online comparing different options and the sites usually give guidance on what the alternatives mean.

There is generally a choice between a gloss or matte cover. This will be a matter of taste and it may be that when you receive the book you feel your choice isn't right. Have a look at similar books to help you make the decision. Matte books have a nice feel to them but gloss books can look more sharp and rich.

Pricing

As with your ebook version, you need to set your price. The platform should calculate your royalty rate based on the print cost of the book and any handling fees or similar that they take. You may have to experiment a little around the price you were hoping to charge in order to ensure your royalty is as you'd hoped. Remember to keep your price at a competitive level rather than maximising royalties by pricing high – people will be less likely to buy your book at an inflated cost. Go through all territories and set sensible figures. If you're using more than one platform, ensure your prices match.

If you are setting up expanded distribution, check you will make a sufficient royalty through those distributed books. If you have the option to set variable wholesale discounts, you can also try different levels until you are happy that you are charging a competitive price but will also receive a sufficient royalty from your sales.

Uploading your files

When you are happy with all the information you have provided for your book, you can upload your files. You will upload the full wrap of your book cover (including your spine and back cover) and a separate interior file. You will then have an opportunity to view a digital proof. Have a careful look through before approving your book and moving on to the next stage.

Proof copies

Always order a proof copy of your book. Even though the digital proof may look great, seeing the actual product is different. You may decide you don't like the finish of the cover, there may be something that looks odd on the print, or you might notice something not quite right in the interior. If you have more than one format, or you've used multiple POD companies, order a proof of each one.

A few days later the proof will drop through your letterbox. I find this part of the process really nerve-racking; there's something slightly terrifying about opening that parcel. Of course, you can use the time to film a book unboxing video (or even live stream it if you're feeling brave!).

Once you've got over the excitement of seeing your book in print, carefully inspect it. At this point, if there are any errors it's still possible to correct them. This is why it's important to do this in good time before the release, otherwise you may find your POD company have already printed copies for presale or distribution and those will carry the errors.

Bulk printing

Obviously, you don't have to use a POD service, and not all indies do. You can order a large print-run of books for a fraction of the per-unit price that POD offers and distribute them yourself. You will have to pay upfront and you run the risk of not selling the books, leading to wasted money and wasted books, but the profit margins are much higher.

You could also use crowdfunding (such as Kickstarter) to help fund the printing cost as discussed in the 'Planning' section of this book. This dramatically reduces the risk to you if the campaign is successful, as well as generating interest in the book ahead of release.

If you do not have storage space, this may not work for you. Also, if you wish to sell in territories outside of your own, this can become tricky – either shipping internationally or paying for printing and storage abroad. But for some, with good marketing to help sell in high volumes, this is a profitable way to work.

Also, POD services may not meet your print requirements. For children's books in particular offset printing may be better suited as it offers more paper weights and finishes. If you want a board book, a lift-the-flap book, or you want more paper stock and finishing options – POD can't handle it.

If this is the case, I would suggest looking into a print run by a local (or overseas) printing company to see if they can offer what you're looking for. You will need to find out about any format requirements they have so you can set up your files as necessary. Ensure you get a proof of the book so you know it meets your standards and there are no errors. Once you have your bulk copies you will have to set yourself up as a distributor to all the sales outlets you wish to use and ship copies to them (or direct to the customer depending on the arrangement). You could work with a distribution company (such as Gardners in the UK) to handle this for you.

An option for UK authors is the company Clays, using their indie publishing branch. They produce short-run prints so while you do have the risk of buying in bulk (although more limited) you also get the associated economies of scale. The good thing with Clays is that they can store your books (depending on volume there is a charge) and, through their partnership with Gardners, can arrange to distribute the books for you.

American indies could use the IAPC (Independent Authors' Publishing Collective). They use printing companies in China for large print runs which can be sent directly to you. They also offer warehousing and distribution for a fee. Again, you benefit from the economies of scale. They generally recommend larger print runs to benefit from the lower cost-per-unit.

* * *

You now have a real physical copy of your book in your hands. It's perfect (hopefully). Your name is written on the cover. Your words are printed inside. You did that! Well done, this is a massive milestone. Cuddle your book in bed (or not).

It's not over yet, though. After all this hard work you don't want your book to vanish into obscurity. Now, you need to actually sell copies and get people to read it. On to the next phase – marketing.

Resources

KDP: kdp.amazon.com
Ingram Spark: www.ingramspark.com
Alliance of Independent Authors: www.
  allianceindependentauthors.org
Barnes and Noble Press: press.barnesandnoble.com
Gardners: www.gardners.com
Lulu: www.lulu.com
Blurb: www.blurb.co.uk
Clays: www.clays.co.uk
IAPC: iapcbooks.com

Marketing

Ideally, you should have left at least six to eight weeks for marketing. This also gives you time to receive and approve your proof copy and to order any author copies you wish to stock. During this time you need to create a buzz about your book to attract sales. Your release day is your best chance to sell a high volume of books (people may start to forget about your book later down the line).

Also, by setting a pre-order phase you generate sales that all count on the first day the books are shipped out. It's possible, if you've chosen your categories well, to enter into bestseller lists on your release day and it's certainly worth a shot.

So, below are a few ideas for things you can do during those final weeks of preparation, although some of them you may choose to start earlier. Think about your book, your skill set and your budget and market accordingly.

It's easy to have your budget run away from you at this point, so be clear on what you can afford and what your priorities are. But, bear in mind that marketing should pay for itself in the number of copies sold.

Don't forget to have fun! In marketing my books I've networked, I've been on the radio and podcasts, I've talked to people I admired about *my book*, I've 'met' people online and, while I've worked hard, I've enjoyed it.

Advance Reader Copies (ARCs)

ARCs can be a useful tool in your marketing strategy. Find people who are relevant to the content of your book and approach them in a friendly email to ask if they would like an ARC. When you contact them, allow plenty of reading time before your release date. You may look for influencers, podcasters, people working in relevant fields and those within traditional media. Look at their platform size – you want your book to reach as many people as possible. However, the 'bigger' the person, the less likely they are to take you up on your offer.

It may seem counter-intuitive to send out free copies of the book, but if these people share it on their social media, talk about it in their media outlets, or write a positive review, it really helps to increase your audience. Some people you send ARCs to may never share anything about it. Others may not take you up on your offer. Some people, of course, may not like your book.

Consider sending ebooks rather than physical copies to save on print costs and postage (although if you are signed up to Kindle Unlimited, you can only do this via Amazon). There are a few good platforms such as Prolific Works and

BookFunnel that make this easy to do. Some readers may prefer a physical copy, and if you feel they are an important ARC reviewer, consider sending them one.

Ask your ARC readers to review the book and share whatever they post. Tell them the release date so they can read the book in time and share their love when it comes out. You may have to nudge them if they forget.

Street team

You could create a street team. In other marketing projects, this might be a group of people physically out in the street promoting something, but books don't really work that way. Look to create a team of enthusiastic people and set up a private Facebook page, WhatsApp group or mailing list to discuss how you are going to create a buzz together. Send them ARCs of your book so they know what they're getting excited about. Give your street team tasks – reviewing your book, sharing your content on their platforms, getting your book into bookshops or libraries – whatever it is you're hoping they will do. Remember to reward them with bonuses such as acknowledgements or access to exclusive content.

Social media

This is one area that should be started before your final marketing push. The beauty of social media is that it's free (unless you decide to use paid ads – more on that later). In my opinion, social media is an absolute must. Depending on which platforms you're comfortable with and your level of skill, choose those you feel you can engage in. Personally, I use YouTube, Facebook, Instagram, Twitter, Pinterest, Goodreads and LinkedIn to a greater or lesser extent. You might like TikTok, Tumblr, Twitch or goodness knows what else! It seems new ones come and go and old ones fall in and out of fashion. Find what suits you and use it.

Start to build an audience by creating content and interacting with other users. Each platform works differently and there's plenty of information out there on how to create a following. In general, nobody likes someone who's just out for the follows – interaction and quality content is key. You have to give and network to get the return. Also, follow-for-follow doesn't lead to interactions. It's best to build an audience organically.

During your marketing phase plan what content you can share to create a buzz. Can you do a cover reveal? Could you share details about how you published the book? Can you run a Q&A? How about providing behind-the-scenes information? Maybe share your inspiration for the book? Can you share relevant content from other creators that feed into what your book is about? Keep on driving people to pre-sales and reiterate how important it is for them to order the book in advance. Share your excitement!

Remember to share your book posts on your personal social media accounts too – your friends will want to know what you're up to, and as long as you don't spam about it, you may well find a loyal, kind audience in the people you already know (and they are more likely to share your content with their own friends).

You need to be comfortable using hashtags. Look for popular ones related to your book, but also smaller ones that aren't so swamped with content. Publicise and follow your own hashtag so people can share content in a way easily spotted by you.

You can use scheduling tools such as Hootsuite or Buffer to maximise the impact of your posts. Have a look at when your audience is most active and set your posts to publish at those times. It also enables you to load up your content in batches if that suits you.

Social media is essentially a free marketing tool, so using it wisely can be an amazing boost to your book visibility and sales. The more your book is out there, the more people will spot it and the more likely those views are to convert to purchases.

Giveaways

Giveaways are a great option to tie into your social media. You could give away the book itself, or associated marketing products. Perhaps you can collaborate with another brand? Crossover giveaways can be really fun and help to boost both your audiences.

My personal opinion is that you should give away something other than the book itself during your pre-sale phase. You might consider making merchandise associated with the book – perhaps prints, bookmarks or maybe goody bags filled with bookish delights? Be creative and keep it relevant to the content of your book.

If you're giving away the actual book, it may make your audience less likely to buy while the competition runs. If you're doing this, end the competition before launch day so that those who did not win can go and order the book.

Make sure that to enter the giveaway people have to follow your social media and share it with other people in some form, whether by tagging them or sharing the post. You want this to get your book out to a larger audience and help to grow your own.

Author website

Depending on your budget, consider starting an author website (although certain free blog-style options work well). An author website acts as a hub for all of your information and provides ways for your audience to contact you.

Make sure people can buy your books on your website, or that it links through to online vendors. Selling on your own website has the benefit of earning a higher royalty for you since author copies are cheap. Offer attractive incentives (such as signed books) if you prefer people to buy through you. While these sales do not add to your rankings, they are more profitable. You also have the option to run pre-orders through your author site if you wish.

Mailing list

Setting up a mailing list is a good idea. By sending newsletters you have direct access to people's inboxes – algorithms can't manipulate that. Decide on the frequency for your newsletters and send out lots of information before your launch (plus a launch day special!). You may want to include exclusive content and giveaways for your mailing list. Remember, this is an audience you can keep for future books, and they're people who were interested enough to sign up; they want to find out more about what you do.

I use Mailchimp for my mailing list, but other options are out there. If you operate in the UK or Europe, you will need to ensure you are compliant with General Data Protection Regulation (GDPR) rules.

Consider giving offers or incentives to get people to sign up to your newsletter. You could have a resource they can access once subscribed or give discounts for goods sold on your website. Also think about adding a pop-up or floating form on your author website.

Paid ads

If the budget allows, you can invest in paid ads for your book. Some people have great success via this route and I think the key is a little experimentation.

If you've published through KDP or distributed through Amazon Seller Central on the Professional Plan, it is easy to advertise your book using Amazon Advertising. Essentially, you bid to get your book in the sponsored spot of a search page. Choose your keywords depending on the search terms you expect potential customers to be using. Set your maximum bid and your total budget and let Amazon do its thing. Your dashboard will tell you how much attention this got your book, how much it cost and whether it translated to sales.

In my experience, Facebook ads primarily work by bringing in new followers, so you're less likely to directly sell books. However, you can get more eyes on your page and people will be seeing your posts about your books. If expanding your audience and reach is what you are looking for, this is worth a try.

Google advertising can be used to drive customers to your website. You can choose to set this to local or global customers. This again works on an auction-style basis, so you set a monthly budget for bids for available ad space. If you want people to be buying products or services from your website, you may find this useful.

BookBub is a useful tool for ebooks. If you're planning to run a discount, you can submit your book to be considered for a Featured Deal. If it's accepted, your ebook will be visible on the BookBub homepage and sent out to curated subscribers (although it's not cheap). Alternatively, by running ads, your book may appear at the bottom of a BookBub email. Similarly to Amazon ads, these run on an auction basis. You set your budget, territory and platform (allowing you to target readers outside of Amazon) and then monitor your sales to see what works. Remember to claim your author profile because followers will be notified of any new releases.

Traditional media

Consider approaching newspapers, radio and TV to be interviewed about your book. Bear in mind that some will view it as advertising and as such may not do this for free, but others will be keen on the content. Local media outlets are more likely to feature you, and you can build a great relationship (personally I like to work with local radio stations). Look for programmes or publications that are relevant to your book or interested in featuring local creatives.

If you are being interviewed live, ask what questions they're planning to ask you, and have a copy of your book handy (always keep a couple wrapped in bubble-wrap in your car or bag – you never know when you might be in a conversation when you wish you could show someone your work).

You could also create an advert to run in traditional media. Investigate the costs for any outlets and then create something suitable if you wish to go ahead with this. Print ads are relatively easy to put together and could attract interest from their readership.

Book trailer

If you have the skills, create a book trailer (or pay to have one made). iMovie is a good free app that's user-friendly if you are an Apple user, but there are plenty of other options. You can upload to YouTube or Vimeo. Have a look at other book trailers for inspiration, but something showing the cover of your book, with snappy information about the content and early reviews over a pleasant piece of music can work well. You can create something more complex if you have the skills.

Share this trailer everywhere. There are people who simply like to watch book trailers so you may find your views on this specific video grow organically.

Q&As

You may like to host livestreams on your own social media platforms answering questions about your book. Ask for questions in advance and filter what you want to answer (it can be embarrassing to have no forthcoming questions, so always best to have some ready).

You might also like to reach out to other authors or influencers about taking part in Q&As and interviews on their platforms as this helps to get your content out beyond your own audience. Again, ask in advance what they're planning to ask you.

* * *

You don't need to do *all* of these things. Find the marketing tools that suit you. Experiment to find what works and try to have fun with it. Marketing can be enjoyable. Remember, the book is done, the bulk of the work is complete, now you just want as many people to enjoy your work as possible.

If you've left enough time for this phase, you can carefully create a hype that should begin to generate sales. Of course, the marketing doesn't end once your book is released; keep on sharing it and promoting it. Use the tools at your disposal to get people to notice your book and, hopefully, to buy it.

Resources

Instagram: www.instagram.com
Facebook: www.facebook.com
YouTube: www.youtube.com
Twitter: twitter.com
Pinterest: www.pinterest.co.uk
LinkedIn: www.linkedin.com
Hootsuite: hootsuite.com
Buffer: buffer.com
BookBub: www.bookbub.com
BookFunnel: bookfunnel.com
Prolific Works: www.prolificworks.com
Mailchimp: mailchimp.com
Vimeo: vimeo.com

Book Launch Day

In my opinion, you should mark your book launch. Months, or even years, of hard work have culminated in this day and doing something to celebrate it feels like a full stop at the end of a sentence (of course, there are still paragraphs to come). You may choose to keep it low-key or plan an event that forms part of your marketing strategy, but I suggest you do *something*. It helps to break the tension of panicking about whether everyone got their orders and what the first reviewers might say.

You might find you feel a bit emotional on launch day. At this point things are out of your hands – your books are out in the world doing the work for you. I'm sure you will have had lots of stressful moments along the way, but I hope you've also had fun and found the process interesting. You might be feeling excited, tired, overwhelmed – probably a gamut of emotions. Or maybe you've breezed through it all and taken the big day in your stride. If so, I'm envious.

When I launched my first book, everything felt surreal, especially as I started to receive reviews and messages from people who'd received their copies of the book. My dream (and a lot of hard work) had become real, and that's an odd feeling. I was glad I had arranged a little book launch with my close friends to help break the tension. One of the best people I know even baked me a cake that looked like my book.

My second book came out in a flurry of hard work as I was preparing to go to a conference where I'd be selling my books. The live stream I'd organised for the day didn't work, essentially because I hadn't tested the system. I spent the day packing and with a migraine. It wasn't quite the same experience as the first time!

Anyway, here are a few ideas for things you may like to do, but be creative! Plan something pleasant or fun to mark the occasion. Many of these suggestions also apply after the launch event and can be used as selling opportunities.

Book signing

Consider arranging a book signing at a local store or library. This could include a reading, Q&A session or other activities (for children's events I like to put out colouring sheets). To arrange a signing, contact the venue and see if they're willing and how they generally go about hosting these events. Often, for lesser-known authors, you supply the books yourself, and this is the best way to ensure they're there on launch day. If the books are being supplied by your POD company to the venue, make sure those distribution channels are set up and the orders will be shipped in time. Keep communicating so you can be sure the orders were accepted and shipped so if there's any hitch you have books to sell. For these kinds of events ask if they would like any artwork (they may even want you to supply printed posters) and share, share, share!

Selling event

You may be able to tie your launch to a book selling event or have a stall at a local or national event. Even better, if this is in some way tied to the subject of your book. Think about creating a buzz – make sure your book is displayed prominently on your table and it's clear that this is launch day! Think about having a takeaway, such as a bookmark, for people who just want information.

Author talk

You could arrange a speaking event with a relevant organisation for launch day. If you feel comfortable with public speaking, this may be a fun way to celebrate. Always practice before the day and have minimal notes so you can talk in an engaging way about your new book.

Online launch event

Using YouTube, Instagram stories or Facebook live, why not host a live event? You could host a Q&A (take a few questions in advance) but always have a few discussion points ready so you're less likely to ramble. You could consider a book reading if you wish to. If you don't like going live online, you could put up a pre-recorded video, although that doesn't give the same exciting vibe.

If you haven't hosted a live event before, make sure you test it out. On certain platforms you can test as a private video to ensure your internet connection and hardware is up to it. Otherwise, you can try a short live event prior to launch to test your system. I have personal experience of having an audience waiting and messaging me while I was unable to get online due to a technical issue.

Online engagement

Encourage people to share your book with you as they receive it. If you use a hashtag, make sure you monitor it – or ask people to tag you in their posts. If you had beta readers and sent out ARCs, ask them to post their reviews on launch day. Don't forget to share all the book love!

Celebrate with friends

Your launch doesn't have to be a public event. Why not have a meal or drinks with a few of your nearest and dearest? You could even go away for a mini-break to celebrate. It can be as big or small as you like. Have something planned rather than expecting others to do it for you (unless they offer) to ensure the occasion is marked as you want it to be.

Final Words

If I can do this, so can you. There may be lots of steps and things to think about and learn, but it is completely within your reach.

You might be doing this yourself, but you don't have to do it alone. Get a writerly community around you (be it virtual or in-person). There are so many people online you can reach out to for tips and support and there are likely to be local authors and writing groups in your area. Self-published and independent authors are generally approachable.

When your book is released, I wish you the biggest congratulations (and please share it with me). It's a huge deal to have come this far. Well done and I wish you every success with your book. Here's to selling numerous copies and receiving lots of wonderful reviews!

Now, on to the next book...

Acknowledgements

Thank you to my editor, Kim Kimber, for being a pleasure to work with for the second time. Also to Steve 'Squidoodle' Turner for the beautiful cover illustrations.

Thank you to my beta readers: Debby Jones, Janice Rosen and Charles Heathcote. I appreciate your feedback and honesty on this project.

Thank you, as ever, to the wonderful indie community for continually supporting one another and happily offering tips and wisdom. I've learned so much from you and I'm glad to be able to contribute. To my subscribers and followers, I am always grateful for your support.

A big thank you to Pete Glass for always being willing to help with Photoshop. To Laura Newing, I'm glad I've found a real unicorn who can even bake book cakes.

Thank you to my husband for supporting my career and encouraging me in writing. Also for helping with the business side of things when I'm completely confused! To my children, thank you for being proud of me, but it's not half of how proud I am of you.

Full list of Resources

The following is an alphabetical list of all the resources mentioned in this book.

Alliance of Independent Authors: www.allianceindependentauthors.org

Apple Books: authors.apple.com/epub-upload

Barnes and Noble Press: press.barnesandnoble.com

BISAC Codes: bisg.org/page/bisacedition

Blurb: www.blurb.co.uk

BookBub: www.bookbub.com

BookFunnel: bookfunnel.com

Books in Print: www.booksinprint.com

Bowker: www.bowker.com

Buffer: buffer.com

Canva: www.canva.com

Chicago referencing manual of style: www.chicagomanualofstyle.org

Clays: www.clays.co.uk

Companies House: www.gov.uk/government/organisations/companies-house

The UK Copyright Service: copyrightservice.co.uk

CIEP (formerly SfEP): www.ciep.uk

Damonza: damonza.com

Domestika: www.domestika.org

Draft2Digital: www.draft2digital.com

Facebook: www.facebook.com

Fiverr: www.fiverr.com

Font Squirrel: www.fontsquirrel.com

Gardners: www.gardners.com

Gimp: www.gimp.org

Google Play: play.google.com/books/publish/u/0/

HMRC: www.gov.uk/government/organisations/hm-revenue-customs

Hootsuite: hootsuite.com

IAPC: iapcbooks.com

InDesign: www.adobe.com

Ingram Spark: www.ingramspark.com

Instagram: www.instagram.com

ISBN International: www.isbn-international.org

KDP: kdp.amazon.com

Kickstarter: www.kickstarter.com

Kindle Create: www.amazon.com/Kindle-Create/b?ie=UTF8&node=18292298011

Kindle Cover Creator: kdp.amazon.com/en_US/help/topic/G201113520

Kindle Kids' Book Creator: kdp.amazon.com/en_US/how-to-publish-childrens-books

Kobo: www.kobo.com/us/en/p/writinglife

LinkedIn: www.linkedin.com

Lulu: www.lulu.com

Mailchimp: mailchimp.com

Nielsen: www.nielsenisbnstore.com

Nielsen Title Editor: www.nielsentitleeditor.com

Photoshop: www.photoshop.com/en

Pinterest: www.pinterest.co.uk

Prolific Works: www.prolificworks.com

Publish Drive: www.publishdrive.com

Reedsy: reedsy.com

Reedsy Book Editor: reedsy.com/write-a-book

Scrivener: www.literatureandlatte.com

Shutterstock: www.shutterstock.com

Skillshare: skillshare.com

Smashwords: www.smashwords.com

Teachable: teachable.com

Twitter: twitter.com

Upwork: www.upwork.com

Vellum: vellum.pub

Vimeo: vimeo.com

The Writers' and Artists' Yearbook: www.writersandartists.
co.uk

YouTube: www.youtube.com

Index

Ingram Content Group UK Ltd.
Milton Keynes UK
UKHW020800270323
419227UK00016B/981

9 781915 289001